A Country
Cook's Kitchen

A Country
Cook's Kitchen

TIME-TESTED KITCHEN SKILLS

*Simple Recipes for Making
Breads, Cheese, Jams, Preserves,
Cured Meats, and More*

ALISON WALKER

Additional recipes by Shona Crawford Poole

with photography by Tara Fisher

RIZZOLI
NEW YORK

New York · Paris · London · Milan

First published in the United States of America in 2012 by
Rizzoli International Publications, Inc.
300 Park Avenue South
New York, NY 10010
www.rizzoliusa.com

Originally published in the United Kingdom in 2012 by
Jacqui Small LLP
An imprint of Aurum Press
7 Greenland Street
London NW1 0ND

2012 2013 2014 2015 / 10 9 8 7 6 5 4 3 2 1

ISBN: 978-0-8478-3839-4

Library of Congress Control Number: 2011938894

Printed in Singapore

Publisher: Jacqui Small
Managing Editor: Kerenza Swift
Art Director: Ashley Western
Project Editor: Abi Waters
Stylist: Caroline Reeves
Photographer: Tara Fisher
Production: Peter Colley

The information in this book is true and complete to the best of
our knowledge. All recommendations are made without guarantee
on the part of the author or the publisher. Please consult the U.S.
Department of Agriculture guidelines for additional information
or clarification: http://nchfp.uga.edu. The author and publisher
accept no liability in connection with the use of the information
in this book.

Contents

Introduction

Think of a traditional country kitchen and what comes to mind? A worn flagstone floor, an old-fashioned Windsor chair sitting snugly next to the warm, welcoming stove… My first thought is of a well-scrubbed, wooden farmhouse table laid out for tea, with feather-light scones, freshly churned butter, soft, creamy cheeses, glistening jars of jam made with berries from the garden—and all homemade, of course.

The kitchen skill needed to make this simple country fare is something our grandmothers and great-grandmothers would have taken for granted, family recipes passed down through generations of women who honed the dishes to perfection. As a child I loved to watch my grandmother making pies: she didn't own a measuring scale or any fancy gadgets; everything was done by touch and experience. And, inevitably, those pies were perfect every time. Sadly, those kinds of skills have now been largely forgotten or fallen out of use because "really, who has the time?" Who needs such things in a modern world where grabbing an inexpensive TV dinner is the norm? That's understandable; of course we're too busy to churn butter or make our own cheese, and why should we when we can pick up perfectly acceptable examples at the local shops? But where's the pleasure in that?

Every now and then, it's good to slow down and reconnect with nature's bounty, enjoy the transformation of raw ingredients into an enticing plate of cookies or mouth-watering layer cake. I will happily spend many an hour turning a crop of just picked raspberries or a basket of hedgerow fruit into rows of jams and jellies to stock the pantry for the winter months, or turn out batches of fresh, meaty sausages for a Sunday cooked breakfast complete with a fruity chutney.

By using modern technology the old-fashioned techniques are easier to revive than you may think. I'm not asking you to laboriously make butter by hand in an antique butter churn (use a food mixer and it takes a fraction of the time) or keep your own pigs in the garden (find a good local butcher instead); just to simply enjoy some of the processes involved in making good food as well as the delicious end result. After all, what cook a hundred years ago would have used a wooden spoon to make a cake if she'd had access to a hand-held electric mixer! It's simple to incorporate country cooking into your life: you could bake a batch of bread for the week, then stock up the freezer with the surplus, while a country walk could turn into a forage for wild plums to make a liqueur to give at Christmas.

Country cooking is close to my heart, the food I most like to prepare and share with family and friends. At its best, it's simple, hearty, thrifty, honest food that is a pleasure to create and a joy to eat. It enables you to cook amazing meals with cheaper ingredients, cope with garden gluts, and, most importantly, know exactly the integrity of the food you are serving. With this in mind, I have covered everything I think the aspiring country cook needs to know, from the perhaps unfamiliar traditional skills of curing, bottling, and cheese making, to the familiar old favorites like cake, bread, and pastry making. Apart from a few recipes, very little specialized equipment is required. Step shots helpfully illustrate some of the trickier skills and each chapter covers in detail the equipment, ingredients, and techniques you might need. My hope is that you will be tempted to delve in from time to time to make a chutney or cake, or to begin to adapt the skills of country cooking to fit your own lifestyle, even if it's only on the weekend. Before long, you, too, can know the pleasure and benefits of eating your own bread, cheese, or smoked fish.

Baking

Baking is surely at the heart of any country kitchen and gives the good cook a chance to shine, even with the simplest of recipes. Who can resist a batch of **freshly baked scones** warm from the oven? The **comforting crunch** of a homemade cookie, a simple supper of fresh bread and cheese, or a layer cake filled with **tangy raspberry jam** is far superior to any store-bought confection. They are a **pleasure to make** as well as to eat, but the secret to success is to remember that baking is an exact science. Accurate weighing and the correct oven temperature are always vital.

Breadmaking

Breadmaking at home is a journey with new avenues and byways to explore at every turn. The more bread I bake, the more fascinating the process becomes. Yet what could be more basic than bread's four principal ingredients—flour and water, salt and yeast? With nothing more added than time and heat, the possible variations of crust and crumb, taste and texture, shape, size, and style are quite literally innumerable.

From grain ground by hand, shaped into flat loaves, and baked on hot stones, bakers down the ages have noted the effects of fire and the type and quality of grain on the end result. Through this, bakers have developed the breads we can choose today. Lucky us, except that for those of us with no decent local artisan bakery, the best we can buy is often factory-made bread. These loaves look good, stale quickly, and will very likely be made with the usual additives that bedevil industrial production.

To bake your own bread is to know what it's made with; and that's just the beginning. Even if you never attempt more than one favorite recipe, every loaf will be subtly different. The heat of the kitchen affects how fast the dough rises—cooler and slower improves flavor. Only you can judge when the dough is ready for the oven. Bake it too soon and the bread won't rise to its full potential. Satisfaction of course is in the eating. How often do we salivate at the instruction: "Serve with crusty bread?" Well here it is.

Left: Brown Tin Loaf.

*Opposite (from top to bottom):
Flowerpot Rolls;
Cheese and Cayenne Breadsticks;
and Walnut and Raisin Bread.*

INGREDIENTS

Flour is the main constituent of bread, usually bread flour, which whether white or whole wheat has plenty of gluten. This is the protein that when mixed with water unravels to form a cat's cradle of elastic strands that trap the gas created by yeast and raise the dough. The more you work with them, the more individual flours become. Even within a single tight category such as organic, stone-ground whole wheat bread flour, the aroma and texture can be surprisingly varied. There are lots of functionally adequate flours available, but some flours are exceptionally fine—perhaps there is one milled locally to you? Check your local area to see if there are any farms or mills producing organic flours—you will really notice the difference.

Rye, oats, barley, spelt, kamut, and other grains can all be milled into flours. None has as much gluten as wheat, and many bake best in combination with it. Fresh is best for flour.

Yeast is the ingredient bakers get most irate about. There are great bakers who swear by compressed yeast and baking gurus who are just as happy with dried. Compressed yeast is pale and crumbles and should be stored in the refrigerator. Stale compressed yeast is darker, fudge-colored, and more plastic. Much of the compressed yeast sold in small wrapped blocks is stale before its expiration date. The recipes in this book use active dry yeast. It is wonderfully reliable and has a good shelf life, but watch the expiration date. Sourdough leaven is yeast in an ancient guise, but that's a whole other story.

Salt brings out the flavor of the bread and keeps the action of the yeast in check. Very little is needed so why not have the best, organic sea salt? If it has large flakes, grind it finely for breadmaking.

Water from the tap is fine in most locations.

Fat is used in small amounts in many recipes. A little butter or oil adds flavor, softens the crumb, and improves the bread's keeping qualities.

EQUIPMENT

Bread's few ingredients need to be measured precisely and an **accurate scale** is essential. When breadmaking by hand, I usually work with 2 pounds of flour at a time, enough to make two to three loaves, so I need a **big bowl**. Earthenware is handsome and traditional. Stainless steel is cheap and, more usefully perhaps, lightweight.

One very simple tool mixes the dough, turns it out, divides it, and cleans the work surface as you knead and when you have finished—a **flexible scraper**. Mine is plastic and I can't work without it. Some breads are baked at the highest temperature your oven can rise to. Fitting it with a **baking stone**, a thick piece of granite, or some other stone that will tolerate 446 to 482°F, allows the oven to hold its heat without dropping when the loaves are first put in. It took me a while to find an affordable stone, but eventually an architectural salvage yard produced a 1¼-inch-thick slab of black granite that is a good fit, and it lives permanently on the middle shelf of one of a pair of ovens. Professional bread ovens inject steam to allow the loaves to rise before forming a crust. Spraying a mist of water into the oven as you put the loaves in is the domestic alternative and needs only a **plastic spray bottle**. **Loaf pans** and **baking sheets** should be heavy duty if they are not to scorch and warp respectively at high temperatures. A **flour shaker**, old or new, is useful. I keep a set of floured **cloths**, untainted by detergent smells, for shaping baguettes. Bowl-shaped **baskets** lined with linen are the real deal for proofing round loaves and earn their keep. And finally, if you are not getting the results you expect, check the heat of your oven with an **oven thermometer**.

A BIT OF TECHNIQUE (KNEADING)

Without a rising agent, in this case yeast, bread would be leaden and indigestible. The purpose of kneading dough is to activate the gluten in flour, helping the molecules of protein to stretch and wrap themselves around the gases produced by the yeast's fast breeding program. There are various ways of doing this, including giving the job to a bread machine or sturdy stand mixer fitted with a dough hook.

I have had success using the traditional British technique for kneading, strenuously pushing and folding the dough with liberal dustings of flour to stop it from sticking. But I have made lighter and better bread since adopting a method of incorporating air into dough made with a higher proportion of water and no dustings of extra flour. If you are prepared to tolerate the sensation of glued-up fingers as the dough turns from a lumpen mess into a mass that is lithe and silky, it is a skill worth cultivating (see page 14).

Yeast works efficiently at temperatures between 77 and 86°F. Too much heat kills it, and at 140°F it dies. Refrigerating dough slows it down sharply, and freezing stops it in its tracks. When warmed up again, chilled or frozen dough carries on from where it left off.

Basic White Dough

Once mastered, this basic recipe will enable you to create a variety of delicious breads and rolls with different toppings and glazes.

PREPARATION **15 MINUTES**
RESTING **AT LEAST 1 HOUR**

Makes enough for 2 medium loaves
**7 cups organic unbleached white
   bread flour**
2 teaspoons active dry yeast
1 tablespoon sea salt
scant 3 cups warm water

1 Put the flour in a bowl and stir in the yeast, mixing it well with the flour. Next add the salt and mix to distribute it.
2 Pour in three-quarters of the warm water and use a scraper to mix, adding the remaining water in one or two batches. As soon as the dough comes together and there is no loose flour in the bowl, turn the dough onto a clean surface to knead. Scrubbed wood is ideal, but any smooth hard surface is fine.
3 Gather together the dough using the scraper and, without flouring the work surface, slide your fingers underneath it, leaving your thumbs on top. Pick up and pull the dough toward your body, lifting your hands to stretch it. Slap it down, throwing it away from you, then fold the dough remaining in your hands over the lower portion, trapping in air. Repeat the action of lifting, stretching, and folding for about 5 minutes until the mixture is

transformed from a sticky mass into a dough that feels alive in your hands. At first you will need to scrape it together from time to time, but as the gluten develops it starts to behave as a single, fairly cooperative entity.
4 Place the dough on a lightly floured surface. Shape it into a ball by bringing the edges to the middle, one at a time, and pressing them firmly into the center. Turn the ball over and tuck it in.
5 To rest the dough and give it its first rise, lightly flour a bowl and put the dough into it, seam-side down. Dust the top lightly with flour to help prevent a skin from forming, cover it with a clean cloth, and place somewhere warm and draft-free for about 1 hour, or until the dough has doubled in volume. Now it is ready to shape, proof (the second rise), and bake.

PREPARATION **15 MINUTES**
RESTING **AT LEAST 1 HOUR**

Makes enough for 2 medium loaves
**3¼ cups organic stone-ground whole
   wheat bread flour**
**2⅓ cups organic unbleached white
   bread flour**
2 teaspoons active dry yeast
1 tablespoon sea salt
scant 3 cups water

Basic Brown Dough

Try experimenting with the proportion of whole wheat to white flour.

In a large bowl, mix the flours and stir in the yeast and salt. Continue as for the White Dough, above.

Flowerpot Rolls

These neat little rolls can be baked in real terra-cotta flowerpots that have been seasoned by brushing with oil and baking several times. Less romantically, and with less fuss, they can be baked in silicone popover molds that look like extra-deep muffin cups.

SHAPING AND PROOFING **ABOUT 1 ¼ HOURS**
COOKING **ABOUT 10 MINUTES**

Makes 12
oil, for brushing
1 recipe rested Basic Brown Dough (see page 14)
2 tablespoons pumpkin seeds, to finish

1 Preheat the oven to 475°F. Brush the inside of 12 small and seasoned flowerpots with oil and set them on a baking sheet, or use silicone popover molds, also set on a baking sheet.
2 Turn the risen dough out of its bowl onto a lightly floured work surface, using the scraper to help it on its way without too much stretching or tearing. Divide the dough into 12 equal pieces. Form each piece into a tight ball by repeatedly bringing an edge to the center and pressing firmly, and drop them into the flowerpots or molds. Cover and proof until almost doubled in volume. Mist the tops with water and sprinkle with pumpkin seeds.
3 Mist the oven (see page 12) and slide in the baking sheet. Reduce the heat to 425°F and bake for 10 to 12 minutes. Turn out of the molds and cool a little on a wire rack. Serve warm.

Walnut and Raisin Bread

This recipe uses the Basic Brown Dough with a little more
yeast to counteract its enrichment with oil, nuts, and raisins.

MIXING AND RESTING **ABOUT 1¼ HOURS**
SHAPING AND PROOFING **ABOUT 1¼ HOURS**
COOKING **ABOUT 20 MINUTES**

Makes 2 small round loaves
1¾ cups organic stone-ground whole wheat bread flour
1½ cups organic unbleached white bread flour
1½ teaspoons active dry yeast
1 teaspoon salt
1½ cups water
2 tablespoons walnut oil
¾ cup freshly shelled walnuts, coarsely chopped
⅔ cup raisins

1 Mix and knead the dough (see page 14). Add the oil, walnuts,
and raisins when the dough is almost ready to rest and
continue kneading until they are evenly incorporated. Form
the dough into a ball and rest in the bowl, covered, for 1 hour
or until doubled in volume.
2 Preheat the oven to 425°F. On a well-floured surface, divide
the dough in half. Form each half into a tight ball and let proof,
seam-side up, in floured linen-lined baskets (or bowls lined with
well-floured cloths), covered, until almost doubled again.
3 Turn the loaves out onto a peel (a long-handled shovel) or
tray (the base of a loose-bottom cake or tart pan makes an
impromptu peel for round loaves and is easier still to use if
lined with a circle of parchment paper. Mist the oven (see
page 12) and slide in the loaves. After 5 minutes reduce the
heat to 400°F and bake for 15 minutes more or until they
sound hollow when tapped.

Brown Tin Loaves

A traditional loaf shape, perfect for toasting. Like many
brown breads, this one is even better the following day.

SHAPING AND PROOFING **ABOUT 70 MINUTES**
COOKING **ABOUT 30 MINUTES**

Makes 2 medium tin loaves
butter, to grease and whole wheat or rye flour, to dust
1 recipe rested Basic Brown Dough (see page 14)

1 Preheat the oven to 475°F. Prepare 2 nonstick loaf pans
(8 x 5¼ x 3½ inches) by buttering them generously. If they
are at all inclined to stick, flour them too.
2 Turn the risen dough out of its bowl onto a lightly floured
work surface, using the scraper to help it on its way without
too much stretching or tearing. Divide the dough in half. Take
one piece and flatten it into a rectangle. Fold one long side to
the center and press it firmly into place. Bring the other long
side to the center and press into place. Fold the long edge
nearest to you onto the farther one and press firmly to seal
the two together. Using your palms, roll the resulting sausage
lightly to fit the pan approximately. Place the dough sausage,
seam-side down, in a prepared pan. Shape the second loaf
the same way. Cover the pans with a cloth and leave them
in a warm, draft-free spot to proof until almost doubled in
bulk—about 1 hour.
3 Dust the top of the loaves generously with whole wheat or
rye flour and make a pattern of diagonal cuts on the tops.
4 Mist the oven (see page 12), place the pans directly on the
baking stone or a baking sheet, and bake for 30 minutes. Turn
the loaves out of their pans and tap them on the base. When
they sound hollow they are done. If you are doubtful, return
them to the oven for a few more minutes. Let cool completely
on a wire rack before slicing.

Whole Wheat Soda Bread

A quick-to-make Irish loaf that uses baking soda rather than yeast as its rising agent.

PREPARATION **20 MINUTES**
COOKING **30 MINUTES**

Makes 1 loaf
1 cup whole wheat flour
1¼ cups all-purpose flour
½ teaspoon salt
2 tablespoons lard
1½ teaspoons baking soda
1 tablespoon cream of tartar
1 teaspoon superfine sugar
1¼ cups buttermilk (see page 78)

1 Preheat the oven to 450°F. Sift the flours into a large bowl, tipping in any bran left in the sifter. Stir in the salt, then rub in the lard. Stir in the baking soda, cream of tartar, and sugar.
2 Make a well in the center and pour in the buttermilk. Quickly mix together with a wooden spoon and tip onto a lightly floured work surface.
3 Shape very lightly into a ball and put on a lightly greased baking sheet. Flatten slightly, then, using the handle of a wooden spoon, mark a deep cross almost two-thirds of the way through. Bake for 30 minutes. Cool on a wire rack. Best eaten on day of baking.

Variations

• If you can't find buttermilk, stir 1 tablespoon lemon juice into 1¼ cups whole milk.
• For a change, add 2 tablespoons mixed fresh chopped herbs, such as chives, parsley, or rosemary, to the flour before adding the liquid.

Cottage Loaf

This loaf is created using the traditional breadmaking method.

PREPARATION AND PROOFING
  ABOUT 2¾ TO 3½ HOURS
COOKING **ABOUT 45 MINUTES**

Makes 1 loaf
3½ cups white bread flour, plus extra
  for dusting
1 teaspoon active dry yeast
1½ teaspoons salt
1 cup hand-hot water
oil, for greasing

1 Put the flour in a large bowl and stir in the yeast and salt. Add the water, mixing quickly as you go—you should have a soft but not too sticky dough. Add a little more water if necessary.
2 Lightly flour a work surface and knead the dough for at least 10 minutes, until it is smooth and springs back when lightly pressed (see page 14). Put the dough in a large, lightly oiled bowl, cover with a cloth, and let rise for 1½ to 2 hours, until doubled in volume.
3 Briefly knead the dough for a couple of minutes to knock out any air pockets, then divide into two-thirds and a third. Briefly knead each piece and shape into a ball. Cover and let rest for about 10 minutes.
4 Preheat the oven to 400°F. Put the large ball onto a lightly floured baking sheet. Put the smaller ball on top and using two floured fingers push down through the center, joining the balls together. Cover and let proof in a warm place for 30 to 40 minutes. To test, lightly press the dough with a finger— if the dough springs back slowly, it is ready to bake.
5 Generously dust the top of the loaf with flour and bake in the oven for 40 to 45 minutes, until golden brown. Tap the bottom of the loaf and listen for a hollow sound—this means the bread is cooked. Cool on a wire rack.

Cheese and Cayenne Breadsticks

These are simple to shape and bake. With no need for butter, they are an easy bite-the-end-off bread for buffets, barbecues, and picnics. Make up your own savory, sweet, or spicy variations to fit what's on the menu.

SHAPING AND PROOFING **ABOUT 45 MINUTES**
COOKING **8 TO 10 MINUTES**

Makes about 20 breadsticks

½ cup fine polenta
1 recipe rested Basic White Dough (see page 14) made with organic unbleached white bread flour
¾ cup Parmesan (freshly grated)
1 teaspoon cayenne pepper

1 Preheat the oven to 475°F. Dust one or more large baking sheets lightly with polenta, and put the remaining polenta in a flat dish.

2 Turn the risen dough gently out of its bowl onto a lightly floured work surface. Shape it into a large rectangle about 16 x 12 inches, lightly stretching the dough into a fairly even thickness. Scatter over the grated cheese, going right up to the edges, and dust evenly with cayenne pepper.

3 Fold one long edge over the middle third of the dough and bring down the other one over the top to make a three-layered dough sandwich.

4 Cut the roll into strips ¾ inch wide, or a little less, using the scraper. Dip the cut edges of one strip lightly in the polenta, then twist it like barley sugar, at the same time pulling gently to lengthen it, and lay it on the prepared baking sheet. Twist up the remaining pieces of dough the same way and lay them side-by-side on the baking sheet, leaving enough space between them to allow for rising. Cover and let proof until almost doubled in volume.

5 Mist the oven (see page 12) immediately before and after putting the breadsticks into the oven. Bake for 8 to 10 minutes, until golden and crisp. These are best eaten the day they are baked, but can be frozen and revived in a hot oven.

Baguettes

As an alternative to using white bread flour alone, try mixing equal quantities of bread and all-purpose flour when making baguettes.

SHAPING AND PROOFING **ABOUT 1½ HOURS**
COOKING **10 TO 12 MINUTES**

Makes 8 baguettes
flour, to shape
1 recipe rested Basic White Dough (see page 14)

1 Lay a floured cloth on a baking sheet, pleating it into ridges and furrows that will hold the shaped baguette, keeping them separate and supported as they proof. Preheat the oven to 475°F.

2 Turn the risen dough gently out of its bowl onto a lightly floured work surface. If you were now to roll pieces of this very soft dough into long sausage shapes, they would flatten and spread and not hold their shape in the oven. So here is how to put some backbone into the dough; the same technique is employed again when shaping the individual baguettes. Without knocking the air out of the dough, spread it into a rectangle. Lift the side nearest to you to the center and press it down firmly. Bring the side farthest from you to the center and press it firmly into place. Now bring the two long edges together and press them firmly together.

3 Divide the dough into 8 equal pieces. Form each one into a ball and flour the top lightly. Let rest for 5 minutes.

4 Spread one ball of dough into a rectangle and repeat the shaping technique in step 2. The final seam will be the underside of the finished baguette. Using both hands and as little flour as possible on the work surface, lightly roll the dough to lengthen it. Carefully lay the shaped dough, seam-side up, into a furrow on the floured cloth. Shape the remainder of the dough balls, dust them lightly with flour, and cover. Let them stand in a warm place to rise until doubled in volume—about 1 hour.

5 I bake these loaves four at a time, and transferring the floppy lengths of dough safely into the oven is the trickiest part of the whole operation. A professional baker would use a peel (a long-handled shovel) and a technique honed with practice. You might find the following method easier. Line a large flat baking sheet with parchment paper and flour it well. Roll four lengths of risen dough onto the prepared sheet, using the cloth rather than your hands to maneuver them, and space them out, seam-side down. Slash each baguette with 5 or 6 diagonal cuts, using a scalpel or razor blade, and a light assured touch.

6 Mist the oven (see page 12) to help form the loaves' crust. Now slide in the loaves on their paper onto the hot baking stone (see page 12), or if you haven't the nerve, sheet and all. Give them another squirt of water, shut the oven door, and bake for 10 to 12 minutes, until the loaves are golden and crisp. If the oven has a glass door you can watch the bread's development as it swells and rises, opening the cuts. This is bread you can eat straight from the oven as soon as it is cool enough to bite without burning your tongue.

A Light Rye Loaf

Increase the proportion of rye to white flour if you prefer a denser loaf.

PREPARATION **25 MINUTES PLUS RISING**
COOKING **45 MINUTES**

Makes 2 loaves
1½ cups white bread flour
1¾ cups rye flour, plus extra for dusting
1½ teaspoons fine sea salt
2 teaspoons active dry yeast
generous 1 cup hand-hot water
½ teaspoon superfine sugar

1 In a large bowl, mix together the white flour, rye flour, salt, and yeast. Make a well in the center and pour in two-thirds of the water. Mix together to form a soft and fairly sticky dough. Add more water if necessary.
2 Turn out onto a lightly floured work surface and knead for 10 minutes, or until smooth and elastic.
3 Put the dough into a lightly oiled bowl and cover with a cloth. Let rise until doubled in volume—about 1 to 1½ hours. Knock back and let rest for 5 minutes, covered with the upturned bowl.
4 Divide the dough in half and shape into 2 loaves about 12 inches long, tapering them slightly at each end. Transfer to a large, lightly floured baking sheet. Lightly dust with rye flour. Using a very sharp knife, make diagonal slashes down the length of the loaves at regular intervals. Cover and let proof for 1 to 1½ hours until doubled in volume.
5 Preheat the oven to 400°F. Bake the loaves for about 45 minutes, until golden. They should sound hollow when tapped on the base. Cool completely on a wire rack before slicing.

Crumpets

Crumpets freeze well and should be toasted after defrosting.

PREPARATION **30 MINUTES PLUS RISING**
COOKING **35 MINUTES**

Makes 12 crumpets
1¾ cups white bread flour
1¾ cups all-purpose flour
2 teaspoons salt
1 teaspoon active dry yeast
2 tablespoons sunflower oil
generous 2 cups hand-hot water
1 teaspoon baking soda

1 Sift the flours into a large bowl. Stir in the salt and yeast.
2 Make a well in the center and pour in the oil and 1¾ cups of the water. Beat until it makes a smooth and elastic batter.
3 Cover with a cloth and leave for 1½ to 2 hours, until the mixture rises and the surface is covered with bubbles.
4 Dissolve the baking soda in the remaining hand-hot water and stir it into the batter. Cover and let stand for 30 minutes.
5 Put a large skillet over medium-low heat. Lightly grease three or four 3½-inch metal ring molds and put into the skillet. Pour the batter into the rings until three-quarters full and cook for about 8 minutes, until the top sets and bubbles have formed on the surface.
6 Turn over in the molds, pushing the crumpet down onto the skillet base, and cook for about 4 minutes, until golden. Keep warm in a low oven. Repeat until the batter is used up.
7 Serve warm with butter and preserves. The crumpets can also be toasted.

Pie Dough

Home-baked savory and sweet pies, delicate pastries, and warming desserts, where would we be without the crumbly, flaky, utterly delicious pie dough encasing them? Before cooks perfected the art of pie dough making, it was simply a vehicle for the filling, something to be tossed away once the middle was eaten. Happily for the country cook, someone long ago discovered how to make featherlight pie dough that deserved to be eaten for its own sake. Some would argue that it's the best bit, and when made well it is a culinary triumph. Don't let that scare the novices among you: follow the steps carefully and you'll discover how achievable and delicious homemade pie dough really is.

A Soggy Base?

Fruit pies often suffer from soggy pie dough bottoms due to their moist fillings. To prevent this: brush the base before filling with lightly whisked egg white to make a seal; or sprinkle 1 tablespoon fine farina on the bottom to absorb juices; or toss the fruit in 1 tablespoon all-purpose flour beforehand.

INGREDIENTS

Low in gluten, **all-purpose flour** is best for pie dough making. **Whole wheat flour** makes a nutty-tasting but heavier dough; use it half and half with white to give lighter results. Good-quality **butter** adds flavor, while **lard** produces a crust that's especially tasty for meat pies. Vegetarians and vegans can replace animal fats with **vegetable shortening.** Adding **egg** to a flaky pie dough mix gives a crumbly rich texture. Beat the egg yolk into the amount of water specified in the recipe before adding to flour: this stops eggy streaks from ruining the appearance of the dough. **Water** should always be ice cold: it ensures that pie dough is crumbly (short) and produces steam for rise in quick puff pie dough. Go easy, though, because adding too much will make it tough. Stir in a little **superfine** or **confectioners' sugar** to add sweetness and color, or a hint of **vanilla extract**, **citrus zest,** or ground **spices,** such as cinnamon, nutmeg, and ginger. **Herbs,** ground **almonds**, **hazelnuts,** and **walnuts,** and **sesame** and **poppy seeds** add texture and taste. A pinch of **salt** is essential to heighten flavor.

EQUIPMENT

Cool hands and **light fingers** are all you need to make good pie dough, but a few other pieces of equipment will make life easier. A **rolling pin** is the most useful: choose from traditional wood or marble, silicone, or glass. There are even antique versions that can be filled with cold water to ensure pie dough is kept cool while rolling. If you plan to make pie dough regularly, invest in a **marble slab** for rolling out—they're inexpensive and stay cool in hot weather. For crisper results, **metal tart pans** conduct heat more efficiently than ceramic dishes. Cookware stores sell ceramic **pie weights** for baking blind, but a mixture of rice and dried beans works just as well. Chill **bowls** and other equipment before you begin, especially in hot weather. Pie doughs can also be prepared in a **food processor**, but be careful not to overprocess.

A BIT OF TECHNIQUE

• Work quickly and lightly and always chill dough after working to relax the gluten and set the fat. It will make the dough easier to roll later.
• When rolling out, use the minimal amount of flour on the work surface and use short, sharp strokes. Give the pie dough a quarter turn every few strokes.

• Chill the pie dough shell thoroughly or freeze until very firm before baking. Don't skip this step: the fat in the dough needs to be very cold so that it doesn't melt in the oven before the pie dough has had a chance to set. If you've watched your pie dough slide down the edges of the pan before, this was probably because you didn't let it get cold enough prior to baking.

LINING TIPS

If lining a pie dish or tart pan, don't try to pick up the rolled-out pie dough in one large piece—it is more likely to split or crack. Instead, roll it loosely around the rolling pin and slide the dish or pan underneath (see pictures, page 28). Carefully unroll the pie dough across the dish, then ease the dough into the pan, pressing it into the corners or edges. At this stage, I like to leave pie dough to sit in the pan for a few minutes before trimming the edges—it allows the gluten to relax, making the pie dough less likely to shrink at the edges during cooking.

BAKING BLIND

When making tarts, flaky pie dough is often baked blind (partially cooked) before the filling is added, otherwise the moisture from the filling would prevent the pie dough from crisping sufficiently, resulting in a soggy base. So the pie dough shell can be partially cooked before a filling is added, then cooked further as in the case of a savory tart; or the case is fully cooked until crisp, cooled and then filled with a sweet filling that needs no further cooking, such as custard or cream and fruit.

To bake blind, line the tart pan with the pie dough as specified above or in the recipe. Prick the base all over with a fork, and line with a crumpled circle of parchment paper that is slightly larger in diameter than the pie dough shell. Fill with enough pie weights to support the sides of the pie dough with a layer in the center to stop it from puffing up. Bake for about 12 to 15 minutes in an oven preheated to 400°F, until the sides are set. Remove the baking beans and baking parchment, then return to the oven for 5 to 10 minutes, until the base is sandy to the touch.

Basic Flaky Pie Dough

As a general rule, flaky pie dough is made with half the amount of fat to flour.

PREPARATION 15 MINUTES PLUS CHILLING

Makes about 8 ounces pie dough
1¼ cups all-purpose flour
a pinch of salt
4 tablespoons (½ stick) cold butter, diced
2 tablespoons cold lard, diced
3 tablespoons ice-cold water

1 Sift the flour into a bowl with the salt. Rub in the fat between your fingertips until the mixture resembles fine breadcrumbs. If the mixture starts to look oily, pop the bowl in the refrigerator and resume when the fat has rechilled.

Sprinkle over most of the water and bring together the mixture into lumps with a flat-bladed table knife. Sprinkle a few drops of the remaining water over any dry areas and bring those together, too. Don't add the water all at once, as too much results in tough pastry.
2 Bring together the lumps with your fingertips and gently knead together to form a smooth disc.
3 Wrap tightly in plastic wrap; chill for 30 minutes before rolling and shaping.
4 Flour the work surface and roll out the dough, giving quarter turns.
5 Roll the dough around the rolling pin, slide the tart or pie pan underneath, and

gently unroll the dough. Ease it into the sides. Trim the edges with a sharp knife and prick the base with a fork. Chill.
6 Line the tart and blind bake following the instructions on page 26 or according to the recipe you are following.

Variations

• To make rich flaky pie dough, use all butter and mix 1 egg yolk with 2 tablespoons ice-cold water.
• To make sweet flaky pie dough, stir in 2 tablespoons superfine sugar after the butter has been rubbed in.

Egg and Bacon Tart

This classic tart is made with just a few simple ingredients. For a change, replace the bacon with smoked ham and the Gruyère with a sharp Cheddar cheese.

PREPARATION **40 MINUTES PLUS CHILLING**
COOKING **ABOUT 1 HOUR**

Serves 6

**1 recipe Basic Flaky Pie Dough
 (see page 28)**
**½ cup diced smoked bacon, without
 rind**
¾ cup grated Gruyère
2 medium eggs, beaten
⅔ cup light cream
salt and freshly ground black pepper

1 Roll out the pie dough and use it to line an 8 inch tart pan. Chill for 30 minutes, preheat the oven to 400°F and then bake blind (see page 26).
2 Turn down the oven temperature to 350°F and put a baking sheet in the oven to preheat. Sprinkle the bacon over the base of the pastry shell, followed by the cheese.

3 Beat together the eggs and cream with plenty of seasoning and pour into the pastry shell. Bake in the oven on the preheated baking sheet for 30 to 40 minutes, until the filling is risen and golden. Serve hot or cold.

Maple Pecan Pie

If you can't find molasses sugar, use dark brown sugar instead.

PREPARATION **35 MINUTES PLUS CHILLING**
COOKING **ABOUT 1 HOUR**

Serves 6 to 8

1 recipe Basic Rich Flaky Pie Dough (see
   page 28) made with 1⅔ cups flour and
   ½ cup (1 stick) cold butter
6 tablespoons (¾ cup) unsalted butter
⅓ cup dark brown sugar
3 medium eggs, beaten
1 teaspoon cornstarch
2 cups pecan halves
¼ cup dark maple syrup
1 cup dark corn syrup
1 teaspoon vanilla extract

1 Roll out the dough and use it to line a 9 inch tart pan. Chill for 30 minutes, preheat the oven to 400°F, and then bake blind (see page 26).

2 Turn down the oven temperature to 350°F and put a baking sheet in the oven to preheat. Beat the butter and sugar together until soft and fluffy, then gradually beat in the eggs and cornstarch.

3 Stir in two-thirds of the pecans, the syrups, and the vanilla and pour into the pastry shell. Arrange the remaining pecan halves on top.

4 Bake in the oven on the preheated baking sheet for about 45 minutes, until the filling is set. Serve warm.

Basic Suet Pie Dough

Suet pie dough is used to make savory and sweet steamed puddings. It is a traditional ingredient that you may be able to order from your butcher. Alternatively, try substituting frozen lard and grate the amount you need. Add a sprinkle of flour after grating.

1 Sift the flour into a large bowl with the salt. Stir in the suet. Sprinkle with 2 to 3 tablespoons ice-cold water and bring together with a flat-bladed knife to make a soft but not sticky dough.
2 If lining an ovenproof bowl, roll out the pastry into a large circle about ¼ inch thick. Cut away about one-third of the dough (as shown above); set aside. Grease the bowl and line with the larger piece of pastry by bringing together the two cut edges so that they overlap slightly (into a bowl shape); press firmly to seal. Add your chosen filling.
3 Roll out the remaining dough into a circle and brush the edges with water. Seal on top of the dough lining and trim. Cover with a lining of wax paper and foil, pleated down the center. Secure with string and trim away the excess paper and foil so that it won't sit in the pan water.

PREPARATION **15 MINUTES**

Makes about 1 pound dough
2½ cups self-rising flour
a large pinch of salt
**scant 1½ cups beef or vegetable
  suet**
butter, for greasing

4 Put the bowl on top of an upturned plate placed in a large pan. Pour in enough boiling water to come halfway up the sides of the bowl, cover, and bubble gently until cooked. Do not let the water boil dry. Alternatively, cook in a steamer. (See individual recipes for cooking times.)

Steak and Mushroom Pudding

PREPARATION **30 MINUTES**
COOKING **6 TO 7 HOURS**

Serves 4

**1 pound 3 ounces braising beef,
   trimmed and cut into bite-size pieces**
2⅓ cups small button mushrooms
½ tablespoon seasoned flour
**1 recipe Basic Suet Pie Dough (see
   page 31)**
1 small onion, finely chopped
½ tablespoon finely chopped parsley
salt and freshly ground black pepper

Once this pudding is on the stove, it will sit happily cooking all day, but check regularly to see if the water level needs topping up.

1 Lightly toss the beef and mushrooms in the flour. Shake off the excess.
2 Line a 1¾-pint ovenproof bowl with two-thirds of the dough (see page 31). Fill the bowl with the meat and mushrooms, layering with the onion, parsley, and plenty of seasoning as you go.
3 Pour in enough water to fill the pastry shell by two-thirds. Seal with a suet dough lid (see page 31). Steam immediately for 6 to 7 hours (see page 31). Turn out onto a serving plate and serve with seasonal vegetables if you like.

Marmalade Steamed Pudding

To vary the recipe, swap the marmalade for jam or mincemeat.

PREPARATION **30 MINUTES**
COOKING **2 HOURS**

Serves 6
zest of 1 orange
1 recipe Basic Suet Pie Dough (see page 31)
1⅓ cups thick-cut marmalade (or for homemade recipes, see pages 104–110)
1 tablespoon whisky (optional)
cream, to serve

1 Stir the orange zest into the dough before adding the water. On a lightly floured work surface, roll out to a 12 inch square.
2 Spread over the marmalade and sprinkle with the whisky, if using.
3 Roll up the pastry tightly from one long end. Cut into ¾ inch slices. Line the bottom and sides of a greased 3½-cup ovenproof bowl with slices of the dough, cut sides outward. Fill the center with the remaining slices. Cover with a layer of pleated wax paper and foil and tie with string. Steam immediately for 2 hours (see page 31). Turn out onto a plate and serve with cream.

Left:
Top left: shape the dough over upturned glass jars;
Bottom: wrap wax paper around the pies to keep their shape while cooking;
Top right: once topped with lids, cut a small hole to let out steam.
Below: the cooked pies are filled with stock.

Basic Hot-Water Crust Pie Dough

Use glass jars, a soufflé dish, or any round straight-sided dish as a mold for the pie dough.

PREPARATION 40 MINUTES

Makes about 8 ounces dough
1⅔ cups all-purpose flour
½ teaspoon salt
¼ cup lard
6 tablespoons water
beaten egg, to glaze

1 Warm a mixing bowl and your chosen mold before using. Sift the flour into a bowl with the salt. Make a well in the center. Put the lard into a pan with the water and bring to a boil. Pour into the well in the flour, then gradually work the flour into the center with a wooden spoon. Beat until combined, then knead until smooth on a lightly floured work surface.

2 Cut off one-third of the dough to make a lid(s) and keep warm by setting on a plate over a bowl of hot water and covering with a cloth.

3 Roll out the remaining dough into a circle ¾ inch larger than the base of your mold and sit the mold in the center. Turn over the mold so that the dough is sitting on the top and then use your hands to mold the pastry down to a thickness of about ¼ inch—the dough should still be warm to make molding easier.

4 Turn over the mold, wrap a double strip of wax paper around the sides, and tie with string. Remove the mold. Add the meat filling. Dampen the inside edge, then roll out the remaining dough to form a lid(s) that sits up to the inner edges. Crimp to seal. Make a hole in the lid to let steam escape. Decorate with dough trimmings if you like. Glaze with beaten egg, chill, then glaze again before baking.

Individual Game Pies

Homemade stock should contain enough gelatin to set in the pie. If using store-bought stock, use 1 teaspoon powdered gelatin following the package directions.

1 Put the game in a nonmetallic bowl with the Madeira or port, mace, and thyme. Marinate overnight in the refrigerator.

2 Mix together the marinated game, sausage meat, onion, and garlic. Season well and chill. Preheat the oven to 400°F.

3 Divide two-thirds of the dough into 6 pieces. While working on one piece, keep the others warm. Roll out and mold around a plastic-wrapped 14-ounce glass jar so they are about 3 inches high. Repeat with the 5 other pieces. Wrap with wax paper and secure. Remove the jars and plasic wrap and fill the pastry shells with the meat, packing in firmly, as it will shrink during cooking (see page 34).

4 Divide the remaining pastry into 6 pieces and roll out lids (see page 34).

Seal the pies and crimp. Cut steam holes and glaze the tops with beaten egg. Chill for 30 minutes.

5 Glaze again with beaten egg. Bake for 20 minutes, then turn down the oven temperature to 350° F. Remove the wax paper, brush the sides with beaten egg, and cook for another 40 minutes. To check that the meat is cooked through, put a skewer into the center of the meat through the steam hole. Hold it there for 10 seconds, then test the temperature on the back of your wrist. If it is hot the meat is cooked; if not return to the oven for 10 minutes and check again. Cool on a wire rack. When the pies are at room temperature, pour in the stock through the steam holes. Let set in the refrigerator.

PREPARATION **40 MINUTES**
COOKING **1 HOUR PLUS OVERNIGHT MARINATING, CHILLING, AND SETTING**

Makes 6 pies

1½ pounds mixed game, cubed, such as rabbit, venison, and pheasant
¼ cup Madeira or port
½ teaspoon ground mace
2 teaspoons thyme leaves
7½ ounces pork sausage meat
½ onion, finely chopped
2 garlic cloves, crushed
salt and freshly ground black pepper
2 recipes Basic Hot-Water Crust Pie Dough (see page 34)
1 egg, beaten
4½ cups game stock

Basic Quick Puff Pie Dough

Make a few batches of this pie dough in one session and freeze any that you don't use. Defrost in the refrigerator overnight before rolling and shaping.

PREPARATION **50 MINUTES PLUS CHILLING**

Makes about 13 ounces dough
1⅔ cups all-purpose flour
a large pinch of salt
6 tablespoons unsalted butter, diced
  and at room temperature
6 tablespoons ice-cold water
6 tablespoons lard, diced and at room
  temperature

1 Sift the flour and salt into a large bowl. Rub in half of the butter until the mixture resembles breadcrumbs.Sprinkle over the water and quickly bring together into clumps with a flat-bladed knife. Bring together with your fingertips and work into a soft but not sticky dough.
2 Shape into a rectangle and wrap in a layer of wax paper and plastic wrap. Chill for 10 minutes to relax.
3 On a lightly floured work surface, roll the dough into a 6 x 12 inch rectangle. Dot half of the lard over the top two-thirds of the dough.
4 Fold the bottom third up to the middle and the top third down to make a parcel. Brush away excess flour on the dough as you do so. Gently mark the edges with a rolling pin to seal.
5 Turn so the long sealed edge is on the left, roll, and fold as before, but without any fat. Chill for 20 minutes.
6 Roll again and dot with the remaining butter as before. Chill.
7 Roll again and dot with the remaining lard as before. Chill.
8 Roll again without fat and chill.
9 Preheat the oven to 400°F. Now the dough is ready to roll, shape as needed, and bake (see recipes opposite).

Sausage and Apple Braid

Use a tart apple to cut through the fattiness of the meat.

PREPARATION **20 MINUTES PLUS CHILLING**

COOKING **55 MINUTES**

Serves 8
1 tablespoon unsalted butter
1 small onion, finely chopped
1 small apple, peeled, cored, and diced
1 pound pork sausage meat
3½ cups fresh breadcrumbs
8 sage leaves, chopped
1 tablespoon grainy mustard
1 recipe Basic Quick Puff Pie Dough (see page 36)
beaten egg, to glaze

1 Melt the butter in a pan and gently cook the onion for about 10 minutes, until softened. Cool. Mix together the cooled onion with the apple, sausage meat, breadcrumbs, sage, and mustard.
2 Roll out the dough to a rectangle ⅛-inch thick. Place the sausage meat down the center. Make horizontal cuts in the dough ¾ inch apart at right angles to the meat.
3 Brush the edges with egg and fold the dough into the center, overlapping as you go. Brush with more beaten egg and chill for 30 minutes.
4 Preheat the oven to 425°F. Place the braid on a heavy baking sheet and brush with more beaten egg. Bake for 15 minutes, then reduce the oven temperature to 400°F and bake for another 30 minutes, until golden. Serve warm, cut into slices.

Spiced Fruit Pastries

Eat these warm from the oven and you'll understand why it's worth going to the effort of making this pastry.

PREPARATION **25 MINUTES**

COOKING **15 MINUTES**

Makes 8 pastries
1 tablespoon unsalted butter
¾ cup currants
1 tablespoon candied citrus peel
¼ cup light brown sugar
½ teaspoon allspice
1 recipe Basic Quick Puff Pie Dough (see page 36)
egg white, to glaze
superfine sugar, for sprinkling

1 Preheat the oven to 425°F. Melt the butter in a pan and stir in the currants, peel, sugar, and allspice.
2 On a lightly floured work surface, roll out the dough to a ⅛-inch thickness. Cut out eight 5-inch circles.
3 Place a spoonful of the fruit mixture in the center of each circle. Dampen the edges of the dough with water and draw into the center, sealing well.
4 Turn over and flatten gently into a round with a rolling pin. Whisk the egg white with a fork until frothy. Brush the tops of the cakes with egg white and sprinkle with sugar. Make 3 diagonal cuts across each cake.
5 Bake in the oven for about 15 minutes, until lightly golden, and eat warm.

Cakes

Surely, there is a cake to suit every mood, palate, and occasion? A slice of featherlight layer cake filled with tangy raspberry jam for teatime, a slab of hearty fruit cake after a bracing winter walk, or a dainty slice of jelly roll at an outdoor summer spread will always please. If it's homemade, so much the better. Simplicity and good-quality ingredients are the key to all the best traditional country cakes, with ornate decoration and fanciful confections saved for special occasions. If you've never attempted to make a cake before, don't be nervous. Take your time, get everything ready, and always read the recipe through at least twice before starting. It really does matter. Take pleasure in the process from the measuring to the whisking and that care will result in a delicious cake. Don't rush and make sure to measure accurately. Even if it sinks in the middle at your first go or looks slightly overdone, a swirl of lightly whipped cream and a scattering of fresh fruit will hide any mistakes—call it a dessert and no one will be any the wiser. I guarantee it will taste better than anything store-bought because it's made with fresh ingredients and lovingly prepared.

INGREDIENTS

The finer the raw ingredients, the more delicious the cake will be, so use quality butter, flour, unrefined sugars, and free-range eggs whenever possible. **Fat** keeps a cake tender and imparts richness and flavor; **butter** produces the finest taste; **vegetable oil** gives a close, dense texture, moist crumb, and good keeping qualities; **vegetable shortening** is flavorless but gives a fine texture.

Sugar sweetens a cake and also helps to keep it tender. **Superfine sugar** is the most suitable for cake making, as it can be easily creamed with butter to incorporate extra air for rising. With their caramel flavors, **darker sugars** are best used for melting-method cakes, such as gingerbread, or creaming-method fruit cakes cooked at lower temperatures. **Corn syrup**, **honey,** and **molasses** may be used as sweetening ingredients but result in a denser, heavier cake because less air can be incorporated during beating.

All-purpose or self-rising **flour** is most commonly used. Never use high-gluten baking flour because it results in a tough, chewy cake. **Cornstarch**, **potato flour**, and **rice flour** add extra lightness. **Eggs** give flavor and color and should be used at room temperature to make them easier to incorporate into the creamed butter and sugar. Cold eggs can be quickly brought up to room temperature in a bowl of warm water for a few minutes. Duck eggs are also suitable for baking and add extra flavor due to the richness of their yolks. Chemical rising agents, such as **baking soda** and **baking powder**, can also be used to help cakes to rise and tend to be included when eggs are added whole rather than separated into yolks and beaten whites. **Baking soda** works with acid ingredients, such as vinegar, molasses, yogurt, sour cream, and buttermilk, to produce carbon dioxide that expands and helps a cake to rise. A pinch of **salt** gives depth of flavor to any sweet mixture.

EQUIPMENT

For successful cake making a selection of **good-quality bakeware** is vital. Always use the size of baking pan specified in the recipe, as it affects cooking times and the thickness/shape of the cake. A **springform pan** is useful for delicate cakes that need careful unmolding. **Silicone bakeware** has the advantage of being rustproof and dishwasher-friendly. A lining of lightly greased **parchment paper** helps stop delicate cakes from sticking and provides protection against oven heat during long cooking times. The correct oven temperature is important, so it is worth investing in an **oven thermometer**. Other essential equipment includes a **flour sifter**, a **wooden spoon**, or **hand-held electric mixer** for beating, and **wire racks** for cooling. A **stand mixer** is useful but not necessary.

A BIT OF TECHNIQUE

• Cakes containing a high proportion of butter (half or more to the weight of flour) are made with the **creaming method**. Cream (beat) softened butter and sugar with a wooden spoon or a hand-held electric mixer until soft, fluffy, and lighter in color. It enables eggs to be beaten in easily and adds more air to aid rise. Suitable for fruit cakes, layered cakes, or loaf cakes. See the Classic Layer Cake (page 42), Dundee Cake (page 43), Chocolate Butterfly Cakes (page 44), Lavender and Lemon Madeira Cake (page 45), Chocolate and Banana Loaf (page 52), and Spiced Carrot Cake (page 53).

• Cakes containing relatively little butter in proportion to flour are made with the **rubbing-in method**: rub fat into the flour to distribute it evenly. A light touch, as with pastry, is needed to avoid producing a tough cake. These cakes are usually egg-free and leavening comes from chemical agents such as baking soda, activated by an acid ingredient. See the Whole Wheat Scones (page 50) and Vinegar Cake (page 50).

• Feather-light **whisked** cakes rely on the whisking process, creating air in the batter while moisture in the eggs and butter converts to steam that expands in the oven. Make them in two ways: whisk whole eggs with sugar over low heat until thick enough to leave a ribbon trail (this gives a softer textured cake); or beat yolks over heat, then fold in flour and whisked egg whites. See the Vanilla and Raspberry Jelly Roll (page 47).

• **Melting method** cakes are the easiest to make: melt fat and sugar together, then stir in eggs and liquid before beating in dry ingredients. Put in the oven as soon as the wet ingredients activate the raising agent. See the Sticky Gingerbread Loaf (page 48) and Honey and Almond Cake (page 49).

Classic Layer Cake

Once you've mastered this basic recipe, vary the filling to suit the occasion: jams and curds for afternoon teas or a fresh fruit compote folded into freshly whipped cream for a special summer party.

PREPARATION **25 MINUTES**
COOKING **ABOUT 25 MINUTES**

Makes 1 (8-inch) cake
1 cup (2 sticks) unsalted butter, very soft, plus extra for greasing
scant 1 cup superfine sugar, plus extra for dusting
a pinch of salt
4 medium eggs, beaten
1½ cups self-rising flour, sifted
1 to 2 tablespoons milk (optional)
3 tablespoons raspberry jam

1 Preheat the oven to 350°F. Lightly grease two 8-inch layer cake pans. Line each base with a circle of parchment paper.
2 Put the butter and sugar in a bowl with a pinch of salt and beat with a wooden spoon or hand-held electric mixer until soft, fluffy, and paler in color. Add the eggs a little at a time while still stirring or with the beaters constantly running, beating well after each addition. If the mixture starts to curdle, beat in 1 tablespoon of the flour.
3 With a large metal spoon, gently fold in the flour, adding, if necessary, enough of the milk to bring the mixture to dropping consistency.
4 Divide the mixture between the 2 layer cake pans and bake in the oven for about 25 minutes, until risen and golden. The tops should spring back when lightly pressed. Remove from the oven and let cool for a few minutes before turning out of the pans onto wire racks and peeling away the paper.
5 Let cool completely, then sandwich the cakes together with jam. Dust the top with superfine sugar. Store in an airtight container for up to 5 days.

Dundee Cake

A light fruit cake characterized by the concentric circles of almonds. It will improve with keeping for a few days.

PREPARATION **35 MINUTES**
COOKING **2 TO 2½ HOURS**

Makes 1 (8-inch) cake
**1 cup (2 sticks) unsalted butter,
  softened, plus extra for greasing
scant 1 cup superfine sugar
grated zest of 1 lemon
grated zest of 1 orange
a pinch of salt
4 medium eggs, beaten
½ cup ground almonds
2 cups all-purpose flour, sifted
1 teaspoon baking powder
1½ cups currants
⅔ cup golden raisins
⅔ cup raisins
1 cup candied citrus peel
½ cup candied cherries
¼ cup milk
⅔ cup whole blanched almonds**

1 Preheat the oven to 300°F. Lightly grease a deep 8-inch cake pan and line the base and sides with parchment paper.
2 Put the butter, sugar, and zest in a bowl with a pinch of salt and beat with a wooden spoon or hand-held electric mixer until soft, fluffy, and paler in color. Add the eggs a little at a time while still stirring or with the beaters constantly running, beating well after each addition. If the mixture starts to curdle, beat in 1 tablespoon of the flour.
3 With a large metal spoon, carefully fold in the ground almonds, followed by the flour and the baking powder. Fold in the fruit and milk.
4 Turn the mixture into the prepared pan and level the surface. Arrange the whole almonds in concentric circles on the top. Bake in the oven for 2 to 2½ hours, until a skewer inserted into the center comes out clean. Cover the top with parchment paper or foil if it starts to brown too much during the cooking time. Remove from the oven and let cool in the pan set on a wire rack. Store in an airtight container for up to 1 week.

Chocolate Butterfly Cakes

Smaller and more delicate sweet morsels than a cupcake, they're a welcome addition to a traditional afternoon tea. Replace the filling with whipped cream and soft fruit for a special occasion.

1 Preheat the oven to 400°F. Place 24 paper cake cases into two 12-hole muffin pans.

2 Replacing 2 tablespoons of the flour with the unsweetened cocoa, make one batch of layer cake batter.

3 Divide the batter between the paper cake cases (about three-quarters full) and bake in the oven for 10 to 15 minutes. Cool on a wire rack.

4 Meanwhile, make the buttercream. Using a hand-held electric mixer, soften the butter with the vanilla, then gradually add the confectioners' sugar and unsweetened cocoa until well blended.

5 Cut a shallow circle from the top of each cake and cut this shape in half to make "wings." Fit a piping bag with a large nozzle, fill with the buttercream, and pipe a swirl into the center of each cake. Arrange the "wings" rounded side down and dust with confectioners' sugar. Store in an airtight container for up to 5 days.

Variations

• Add 1 teaspoon grated lemon or orange zest to the plain cake mixture.
• For a citrus buttercream, omit the cocoa and add 1 to 2 teaspoons lemon or orange juice to taste.

PREPARATION **35 MINUTES**
COOKING **10 TO 15 MINUTES**

Makes 24
1 recipe Classic Layer Cake mixture (see page 42), made with 2 tablespoons sifted alkalized unsweetened cocoa
confectioners' sugar, for dusting

FOR THE BUTTERCREAM FROSTING
½ cup (1 stick) unsalted butter, softened
a few drops of vanilla extract
2 cups confectioners' sugar, sifted
1 tablespoon alkalized unsweetened cocoa, sifted

Lavender and Lemon Madeira Cake

Simply omit the lavender for a classic version of this cake.

PREPARATION **35 MINUTES**
COOKING **1 ¼ HOURS**

Makes 1 (6½-inch) cake
¾ cup (1½ sticks) unsalted butter, softened, plus extra for greasing
⅞ cup lavender sugar (see page 96)
grated zest and juice of 1 lemon
a pinch of salt
3 medium eggs, beaten
¾ cup self-rising flour
⅓ cup ground almonds
milk (optional)

FOR THE FROSTING
2 sprigs fresh or dried lavender
⅔ cup confectioners' sugar, sifted
1 tablespoon lemon juice

1 Lightly grease a 6½-inch cake pan and line the base with a circle of parchment paper. Preheat the oven to 325°F.
2 Put the butter and sugar in a bowl with the lemon zest and salt and beat with a wooden spoon or a hand-held electric mixer until soft, fluffy, and paler in color. Add the eggs a little at a time while still stirring or with the beaters constantly running, beating well after each addition. If the mixture starts to curdle, beat in 1 tablespoon of flour. Add the lemon juice.
3 With a large metal spoon, gently fold in the flour and almonds, adding, if necessary, a drop of milk to bring the mixture to dropping consistency. Spoon into the cake pan and bake in the oven for about 1¼ hours, until risen and golden. The top should spring back when lightly pressed with a finger. Remove from the oven and let cool for a few minutes before turning out of the pan onto a wire rack and peeling away the paper.
4 Meanwhile, make the frosting. Strip the lavender flowers from their stalks if using fresh and put into a bowl with the rest of the frosting ingredients. Mix until smooth—the mixture should thickly coat the back of a spoon. If necessary, add warm water drop by drop until the desired consistency is achieved.
5 When the cake has cooled completely, pour over the frosting and let set before serving. Decorate with fresh lavender sprigs if you like. Store in an airtight container for up to 5 days.

Vanilla and Raspberry Jelly Roll

The filling could be replaced with a few tablespoons of jam or fruit compote, or make a chocolate version by swapping half of the flour for unsweetened cocoa.

1 Preheat the oven to 425°F. Grease a 13 x 9 inch jelly roll pan and line the base with greased parchment paper. Dust with superfine sugar, then flour. Tap out the excess.
2 To make the jelly roll, whisk the eggs and ½ cup of the sugar in a large bowl until the mixture is thick and pale—the whisk should leave a trail for a few seconds when lifted out.
3 Using a large metal spoon, gently but quickly fold the flour and baking powder into the mixture using a figure eight movement.
4 Pour the mixture into the pan, gently knocking out any flour pockets with the spoon if necessary. Level the mixture, spreading it out into the corners. Bake for 5 to 6 minutes, until golden and the cake shrinks from the edges of the pan.
5 Meanwhile, put a piece of parchment paper slightly larger than the cake on the work surface. Sprinkle with the remaining superfine sugar.
6 Turn the cake out onto the sugared paper. Remove the pan and carefully peel away the paper. Trim the edges of the cake to neaten and make a light score mark 1 inch in from one short edge. Using the paper under the cake to help, roll up the cake tightly from the scored short end. Leave it rolled up while it cools.
7 To make the filling, lightly whip the cream with the vanilla and confectioners' sugar until it just holds its shape. Gently fold in the raspberries.
8 To assemble the jelly roll, unroll the cake and spread with the cream mixture. Reroll tightly and put on a serving plate or board. Cut into slices to serve and eat within 3 days.

PREPARATION **35 MINUTES**
COOKING **5 TO 6 MINUTES**

Makes 1 (9-inch) jelly roll
butter, for greasing
¾ cup superfine sugar, plus extra
for dusting
⅔ cup all-purpose flour, sifted, plus
extra for dusting
3 medium eggs
1 teaspoon baking powder

FOR THE FILLING
1 cup heavy cream
1 teaspoon vanilla extract
2 tablespoons confectioners' sugar,
sifted
1 cup fresh raspberries

Sticky Gingerbread Loaf

This gingerbread improves with age, becoming more deliciously sticky after a few days. Wrap in wax paper and store in an airtight container.

PREPARATION **25 MINUTES**
COOKING **ABOUT 1 HOUR**

Makes 1 (2-pound) loaf cake
6 tablespoons (¾ stick) unsalted butter, plus extra for greasing
½ cup dark brown sugar
⅓ cup molasses
½ cup milk
1 cup all-purpose flour
1 teaspoon ground ginger
1 teaspoon ground cinnamon
1 teaspoon baking soda
1 medium egg, beaten
2 balls preserved ginger, roughly chopped, plus 2 tablespoons of the syrup

1 Preheat the oven to 300°F. Lightly grease a 2-pound loaf pan and line the base and sides with parchment paper.
2 Melt the butter, sugar, and molasses in a saucepan over low heat until the sugar is dissolved. Stir in the milk and let cool a little.
3 Sift together the flour, spices, and baking soda. Quickly beat into the melted butter mixture along with the egg, preserved ginger, and syrup, making sure there are no pockets of flour, and turn into the prepared loaf pan.
4 Bake in the oven for about 1 hour—cover the top with a piece of parchment paper if it starts to brown too much. The gingerbread is cooked when a skewer inserted in the center comes out clean. Remove from the oven and let cool on a wire rack.

Honey and Almond Cake

Experiment with different types of honey for subtle flavor changes.

PREPARATION **35 MINUTES**
COOKING **1¼ HOURS**

Makes 1 (8-inch) cake
6 tablespoons (¾ stick) unsalted butter, plus extra for greasing
1 cup clear orange blossom honey, plus 3 tablespoons, to finish
1¾ cups whole wheat flour
⅓ cup ground almonds
1 teaspoon allspice
1 teaspoon baking soda
3 medium eggs, beaten
3 tablespoons milk
grated zest of 1 orange
⅓ cup flaked almonds, to decorate

1 Preheat the oven to 325°F. Lightly grease and line the base and sides of a 8-inch square cake pan with parchment paper. Put the honey and butter in a saucepan and heat gently to melt together. Let cool slightly.
2 Sift the flour, almonds, allspice, and baking soda into a large bowl.
3 Stir the eggs, milk, and orange zest into the honey. Make a well in the center of the flour and pour in the honey mixture. Quickly blend the ingredients together, then pour into the prepared pan. Sprinkle over the almonds and bake for 1¼ hours, until a skewer inserted into the center comes out clean.
4 While the cake is still hot, prick with a skewer and drizzle over the honey-butter mixture. Let cool in the pan for 10 minutes, then turn out onto a wire rack. Store in an airtight container for up to 1 week.

Whole Wheat Scones

Scones are best eaten on the day they're made and are delicious warm from the oven.

PREPARATION **15 MINUTES**
COOKING **12 TO 15 MINUTES**

Makes 6 to 8 scones
⅞ **cup self-rising white flour**
¾ **cup self-rising whole wheat flour**
1 teaspoon baking powder
a pinch of salt
3 tablespoons cold unsalted butter,
 diced, plus extra for greasing
⅔ **cup milk or buttermilk**
beaten egg, to glaze
butter, cream or jam, to serve

1 Preheat the oven to 425°F. Sift the flours and baking powder into a large bowl with the salt. Rub in the butter until the mixture resembles fine breadcrumbs. Alternatively, blend in a food processor, then transfer to a bowl.
2 Using a flat-bladed table knife, gradually work in enough milk to form a soft but not too sticky dough.
3 Turn onto a lightly floured work surface and knead briefly to bring the dough together—overhandling will make the scones tough. Lightly press out to a 1-inch thickness and cut out rounds with a 2½-inch cutter. Reroll the trimmings if you like, but they won't be quite as light.
4 Put the scones on a lightly greased baking sheet, spaced well apart, and brush the tops with the egg—try not to let the egg run down the sides, as it will inhibit the scones from rising. Bake for 12 to 15 minutes, until well risen and golden. Transfer to a wire rack to cool. Serve warm or at room temperature, split in half and spread with butter or cream and jam.

Variations

• **Plain:** replace the whole wheat flour with the same amount of white self-rising flour.
• **Fruit:** Add 3½ ounces raisins and 1 tablespoon superfine sugar to the rubbed in mixture before adding the milk.
• **Cheese:** Add 3½ ounces grated sharp Cheddar and a pinch each of cayenne pepper and English mustard powder after the butter is rubbed in.

Vinegar Cake

This egg-free cake has a lighter texture than most fruit cakes, and you won't be able to detect the vinegar!

PREPARATION **30 MINUTES**
COOKING **2 HOURS**

Makes 1 (9-inch) cake
1 cup (2 sticks) unsalted butter, diced,
 plus extra for greasing
¾ **cup all-purpose flour, sifted**
1⅛ **cups light brown sugar**
1 cup golden raisins
1 cup dried apricots, chopped
1 cup dried cranberries
1 teaspoon baking soda
1¼ **cups milk**
3 tablespoons malt or distilled vinegar

1 Preheat the oven to 400°F. Lightly grease and line the base and sides of a deep 9-inch cake pan with parchment paper.
2 Rub the butter into the flour until the mixture resembles fine breadcrumbs. Stir in the sugar and dried fruit.
3 Mix together the remaining ingredients in a separate bowl. Stir immediately into the flour mixture until combined.
4 Pour into the prepared cake pan and bake in the oven for 30 minutes. Turn down the oven temperature to 325°F and bake for another 1½ hours, or until a skewer inserted into the center of the cake comes out clean. If the top starts to brown too much, cover with a piece of foil.
5 Let cool in the pan for 20 minutes, then turn out onto a wire rack to cool completely. Store in an airtight container for up to 1 week.

Chocolate and Banana Loaf

This is also good when made with a flavored chocolate, such as ginger or butterscotch.

PREPARATION **35 MINUTES**
COOKING **45 TO 50 MINUTES**

Makes 1 (2-pound) loaf cake
1 stick unsalted butter, melted and cooled, plus extra for greasing
2⅛ cups all-purpose flour
scant ½ cup alkalized unsweetened cocoa
4 teaspoons baking powder
1 teaspoon baking soda
3 large bananas, mashed
¾ cup superfine sugar
3 medium eggs, beaten
6 ounces dark chocolate, chopped

1 Preheat the oven to 375°F. Lightly grease and line a 2-pound loaf pan with parchment paper. Sift the flour, unsweetened cocoa, baking powder, and baking soda in a large bowl.
2 Stir together the bananas, sugar, eggs, and butter. Fold in the flour mixture, followed by the chocolate.

3 Turn into the prepared pan, smooth the top, and bake in the oven for 45 to 50 minutes, until a skewer inserted into the center comes out clean. Let cool in the pan for 5 minutes before turning out onto a wire rack. Store in an airtight container for up to 1 week.

Spiced Carrot Cake

Once frosted, this cake will keep in the refrigerator for up to 5 days.

PREPARATION **30 MINUTES**
COOKING **50 TO 60 MINUTES**

Makes 21 pieces

1¼ cups sunflower oil, plus extra for greasing
1¼ cups self-rising white flour, sifted
⅔ cup self-rising whole wheat flour, sifted
3 cups superfine sugar
2 teaspoons baking powder
⅔ cup roughly chopped walnuts
1 tablespoon allspice
2 teaspoons ground ginger
4 medium eggs
1 teaspoon vanilla extract
5 cups grated carrots

FOR THE FROSTING
½ cup (1 stick) unsalted butter, softened
⅞ cup confectiners' sugar, sifted
1¾ cups cream cheese, softened
1 tablespoon runny honey, plus extra for drizzling
juice of half a lemon

1 Preheat the oven to 400°F. Lightly grease and line a 12 x 9 inch cake pan with parchment paper.
2 Put all of the dry ingredients into a large bowl. Stir to combine. Beat the eggs into the oil with the vanilla.
3 Make a well in the center of the flour and pour in the eggs and oil along with the carrots. Mix together quickly, then pour into the prepared pan.
4 Bake for 50 to 60 minutes, or until risen and golden. Cool in the pan for 10 minutes, then turn onto a wire rack.
5 Beat together the frosting ingredients until smooth and chill until thickened. Spread the frosting over the cake and drizzle with honey before serving.

Cookies and Bars

It should be a rule that every country kitchen owns a slightly battered tin brimming with homemade cookies ready to offer with coffee to unexpected guests or simply for the pure enjoyment of your own snacks. Cookie making is one of the easiest of the baking arts to master but no less pleasurable for that. Half an hour or so in the kitchen is all it takes to produce a batch of tempting delights: crumbly shortbread; chunky cookies; oatcakes to enjoy with cheese; sweet or savory; crunchy or gooey; plain or lavish. The variety is endless but the necessary basic ingredients are few. A sprinkling of nuts or chocolate are welcome embellishments, but even the plainest recipe will delight when enjoyed with a nice cup of tea and a sit down.

INGREDIENTS

A delicious cookie can be created with just a few simple pantry ingredients, like **butter**, **sugar**, **flour**, and **eggs**. But once that basic recipe is mastered, a whole range of ingredients may be added to create endless flavor and texture combinations. **Rice flour** produces a lighter, more crumbly texture; **farina** gives a light crunch, while **ground almonds** or **hazelnuts** impart a delicate nuttiness. **Ground spices** bring warmth and depth; darker, **unrefined sugars** color and give a fuller flavor; unsweetened cocoa or **chocolate chips** add delightful indulgence. **Honey** and **molasses** give extra sweetness and depth of flavor and marry very well with aromatic spices, like **cinnamon**, **nutmeg**, and **ginger**. Firm syrup doughs, such as **gingerbread**, are robust enough to roll into large sheets suitable for baking and making into gingerbread houses. **Flavored sugars**, such as lavender, vanilla, and cinnamon, come into their own, while grated **citrus zest** is a welcome but subtle addition. **Oats**, **wheatgerm**, and **whole wheat** flours give a healthy, nutty dimension to savory cookies. For a pleasing contrasting texture, crunchy cookies can be sandwiched with creamy, flavored **buttercreams** or decorated with **glacé** or **royal frosting**.

EQUIPMENT

Little is needed in the way of specialized equipment. A basic creamed cookie mixture can be created with a **wooden spoon**, a **bowl**, and a lot of **elbow grease**. However, a **hand-held electric mixer** or a **stand mixer** will make life easier and enable you to expand your repertoire quickly. Invest in flat and heavy, light-colored **cookie sheets**, which conduct heat more evenly. A **wire rack** is essential for cooling cookies and stops the bottoms from becoming soggy. A **rolling pin**, **metal palette knife**, and **pastry brush** are useful. A **piping bag** will allow you to create fanciful shapes. **Cookie cutters** come in many shapes and sizes, from plain and fluted to festive and themed, such as animals or letters. Invest in them as and when you please; they are not essential. For simple rounds, the rim of a glass is sufficient for stamping out shapes. Very precise shapes can be achieved with a **cookie press**: it comprises a metal cylinder with interchangeable discs, which is filled with creamed dough mixture. The mixture is pressed through the holes in the disc to make a pattern. However, the cookies tend to be small and are more suitable for serving as petit fours.

Parchment paper gives excellent antisticking properties and is best for lining cookie sheets when making cookies with a high sugar content (don't use wax paper, as the cookies will be more likely to stick). Alternatively, rolls of **silicone liners**, available from good cookware store, can be cut to the size of your cookie sheets, washed, and used again and again.

Dedicated cookie makers should rummage in antique and vintage stores, and markets for **carved wooden rolling pins**, known in Germany as *springerle*. A tradition in many northern European countries and especially used at Christmastime, they are carved with elaborate designs and rolled across cookie dough to imprint a pattern before baking.

A BIT OF TECHNIQUE

- Like pie dough making, a light touch is essential when rubbing in fat, working in flour, or rolling out dough to avoid tough or heavy cookies.
- Flour work surfaces sparingly when rolling, as too much will make cookies overdry. Only roll dough out once for the same reason.
- Avoid overbeating a creamed mixture when adding egg—too much air produces cookies with a cakelike texture.
- If the mixture overspreads during baking, the proportion of fat or sugar is too high; bake a test cookie first if in doubt.
- Once cooked, leave the cookies on the cookie sheet for 1 to 2 minutes until firm enough to transfer to a wire rack to cool completely before transferring to an airtight container.
- Don't store cookies in the same containers as cake because they will soften and taste stale. Layer sticky cookies with sheets of wax paper.
- Most cookies will last for about 5 days in an airtight container after baking; cookies high in fat, such as shortbread, or those with a low moisture content, such as biscotti, will keep for up to 1 month. Alternatively, freeze, making sure they are well wrapped, for up to 1 month.
- Slightly stale cookies can be revived in the oven at 300°F for 5 minutes.

From left to right:
Vanilla Shortbread (page 61)
Peanut Butter and Raisin Cookies (page 60)
Almond Macaroons (page 60)
Refrigerator Cookies (page 61)

Peanut Butter and Raisin Cookies

A cookie more suitable for adult tastes, combining sweet raisins and savory peanut butter: use an unsweetened version if you prefer a less sweet result.

PREPARATION **20 MINUTES**

COOKING **15 MINUTES**

Makes 12 cookies

9 tablespoons unsalted butter, softened, plus extra
  for greasing
¾ cup superfine sugar
1 medium egg
½ cup crunchy peanut butter
1 cup all-purpose flour, sifted
½ teaspoon baking powder
1 cup raisins

1 Preheat the oven to 375°F and lightly grease 2 cookie sheets. Cream together the butter and sugar until light and fluffy. Beat in the egg until combined, followed by the peanut butter.
2 Add the flour and baking powder and stir to combine. Add the raisins.
3 Drop dessertspoons of the mixture onto the cookie sheets, spacing well apart to allow for spreading. Bake in the oven for 15 minutes. Let cool on the cookie sheets for 2 minutes, then transfer to a wire rack to cool completely. Store in an airtight container for up to 5 days.

Almond Macaroons

Macaroons are traditionally made on rice paper, but if it is difficult to get hold of, you can line baking sheets with parchment paper as an alternative.

PREPARATION **15 MINUTES**

COOKING **20 TO 25 MINUTES**

Makes 16 macaroons

8 whole blanched almonds
2 large egg whites
⅞ cup ground almonds
⅞ cup superfine sugar
⅕ cup rice flour
¼ teaspoon almond extract

1 Preheat the oven to 325°F. Line 2 baking sheets with rice or parchment paper. Split the almonds in half lengthwise.
2 Whisk the egg whites in a large bowl until they form soft peaks.
3 Fold in the ground almonds, superfine sugar, rice flour, and almond extract.
4 Put teaspoons of the mixture onto the baking sheet and press down slightly with the back of a spoon. Place an almond half in the center. Bake in the oven for 20 to 25 minutes, until lightly golden. Let set on the baking sheet for 2 minutes to set, then transfer to a wire rack to cool. Cut around the rice paper, if using, before storing in an airtight container for up to 5 days.

Vanilla Shortbread

Don't panic if the mixture seems too crumbly—pressing it on the baking sheet will ensure it sticks together for baking.

PREPARATION **20 MINUTES**

COOKING **20 TO 30 MINUTES**

Makes 6 to 8 pieces

9 tablespoons unsalted butter, diced, plus extra for greasing

⅞ cup all-purpose flour

scant ½ cup rice flour

⅓ cup vanilla sugar (see below)

1 Preheat the oven to 350°F and lightly grease a baking sheet.

2 Sift both flours into a large bowl and stir in the sugar. Rub in the butter until the mixture is crumbly and the fat is evenly distributed.

3 Lightly knead the mixture into a ball—don't use any liquid as the moisture from the butter should be sufficient.

4 Dust the work surface with rice flour and press the ball into an 8-inch round (or press into a shortbread mold). Crimp the edges with your fingers, then transfer to the baking sheet. Chill for 30 minutes.

5 Score the surface into wedge-shaped portions, then prick all over with a fork. Bake in the oven for 20 to 30 minutes, until the shortbread feels firm to the touch and is lightly golden in color. Let set for a few minutes before transferring to a wire rack to cool. When cooled, slice into wedges using the score marks as your guide. Store in an airtight container for up to 1 week.

Tip

Save used vanilla beans from making ice cream or custard to create your own vanilla sugar. Rinse and dry the empty pods and bury 1 or 2 split vanilla beans in a large jar of superfine sugar. Let infuse for 2 weeks before using.

Refrigerator Cookies

The dough can be frozen as a log or kept in the refrigerator for up to 2 weeks and slices cut and baked when needed.

PREPARATION **20 MINUTES**

COOKING **8 TO 10 MINUTES**

Makes 30 to 40 cookies

9 tablespoons unsalted butter, softened, plus extra for greasing

⅔ cup superfine sugar

1 medium egg

1 teaspoon vanilla extract

1¾ cups all-purpose flour, sifted

¼ teaspoon baking powder

a pinch of salt

1½ tablespoons alkalized unsweetened cocoa

1 egg white, lightly beaten with a fork

1 Cream together the butter and sugar until light and fluffy. Beat in the egg and vanilla until combined.

2 Combine the flour, baking powder, and salt with the butter mixture using a wooden spoon. Bring together with your hands if it becomes too stiff to work with the spoon.

3 Divide the mixture into 2 portions and work the unsweetened cocoa into one half. Wrap each portion in plastic wrap and chill for 30 minutes.

4 Lightly flour the work surface and roll out each piece of dough into a rectangle ⅛-inch thick. Trim to make both rectangles the same size.

5 Brush the light dough with egg white and place the dark dough on top. Brush the top with more egg white. Starting at one of the long sides, roll both layers of the dough together into a long sausage shape. Wrap in plastic wrap and chill until firm.

6 Preheat the oven to 375°F and lightly grease 2 baking sheets. Cut the dough into ¼-inch slices and place them on the greased baking sheets, leaving at least 2 inches between each one to allow for spreading. Bake in the oven for 8 to 10 minutes, until lightly golden and firm to the touch. Let cool on the baking sheets for 2 minutes, then transfer to a wire rack to cool completely. Store in an airtight container for up to 5 days.

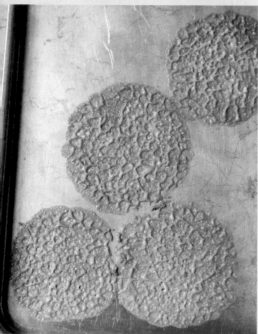

Brandy Snaps

Don't be tempted to cook too many at once as they will harden before you have time to mold them around the wooden spoons.

PREPARATION **20 MINUTES**
COOKING **30 MINUTES**

Makes 12 to 15 brandy snaps
6 tablespoons (¾ stick) unsalted butter, plus extra for greasing
flavorless oil, for greasing
⅓ cup superfine sugar
3 tablespoons dark corn syrup
½ cup all-purpose flour
1 teaspoon ground ginger
2 tablespoons brandy
juice of half a lemon
cream, to serve (optional)

1 Preheat the oven to 375°F and lightly grease 2 baking sheets. Lightly oil the handles of 2 or 3 wooden spoons.
2 Melt the butter, sugar, and corn syrup in a pan set over low heat until combined. Let cool for a few minutes.
3 Sift together the flour and ground ginger, then beat into the butter mixture with the brandy and lemon juice.
4 Put tablespoons of the mixture onto the baking sheets, spacing well apart to allow for spreading. You will need to bake the mixture in batches. Bake in the oven for 8 to 10 minutes, until golden brown with a lacy texture.
5 Let the brandy snaps sit on the baking sheet for 10 seconds or so to firm up slightly. Working quickly, remove the brandy snaps with a palette knife and roll them around the wooden spoon handles. Transfer to a wire rack to cool and remove from the spoons as soon as they are set. If the brandy snaps harden before you have time to roll them, pop them back in the oven for a few seconds to resoften.
6 Store in an airtight container for up to several days. Fill with lightly whipped cream if you like, just before serving.

Florentines

A touch of spice adds a seasonal flavor to these Florentines.

PREPARATION **30 MINUTES**
COOKING **30 MINUTES**

Makes about 50 florentines
4 tablespoons (½ stick) unsalted butter
6 tablespoons heavy cream
½ cup granulated sugar
¾ cup flaked toasted almonds
⅔ cup chopped toasted hazelnuts
½ cup candied cherries, chopped
⅔ cup candied orange peel, finely chopped
finely grated tangerine zest
½ teaspoon ground cinnamon
½ nutmeg, grated
⅓ cup all-purpose flour
¼ teaspoon salt
2 cups dark chocolate

1 Preheat the oven to 350°F. Line 2 or more baking sheets with parchment paper, or use nonstick sheets or silicone liners.
2 Put the butter, cream, and sugar in a heavy-bottom pan and heat slowly, stirring until the sugar dissolves. Bring the mixture to a boil, then remove the pan from the heat and stir in the almonds, hazelnuts, cherries, candied peel, tangerine zest, cinnamon, nutmeg, flour, and salt.
3 Drop teaspoons of the mixture onto the prepared sheets, spacing them well apart to allow for spreading. Use a wet knife to flatten each one, then bake in the oven for 8 to 10 minutes, until they begin to brown at the edges. While still warm, transfer to a wire rack and let cool.
4 Break the chocolate into a large bowl and set it over a small pan of water that has just boiled and been taken off the heat. Let the chocolate warm slowly, stirring until it is fully melted. Alternatively, melt it in a microwave. Spread the smooth underside of each florentine with the melted chocolate, then set them back on the racks, chocolate side up, and let harden.
5 When cooled, store the florentines in an airtight container for up to 1–2 weeks.

Thyme Oatcakes

Swap the thyme for rosemary or omit the herbs altogether if you prefer a plain oatcake. Perfect served with your favorite cheese and chutney.

PREPARATION **20 MINUTES PLUS STANDING**
COOKING **20 TO 30 MINUTES**

Makes 16 oatcakes
⅞ cup medium rolled oats, plus extra for rolling
1 teaspoon chopped thyme leaves
a pinch of salt
1 tablespoon butter or lard, diced
½ cup boiling water

1 Preheat the oven to 350°F and line 2 baking sheets with parchment paper.
2 Put the oats in a bowl and stir in the thyme leaves with a pinch of salt.
3 Add the butter or lard to the boiling water. Once melted, stir this into the oats and let stand for 5 minutes.
4 When cool enough to handle, bring the oats together into a dough and knead briefly. Dust the work surface with oats and roll out to a ⅛-inch thickness. Stamp out rounds with a 2½-inch round cutter and transfer to the baking sheets. Bake in the oven for 20 to 30 minutes. Cool on a wire rack. Store in an airtight container for up to 1 week.

Fruit and Mixed Seed Bars

These simple bars are easy to adapt with your favorite dried fruit and seeds—just keep the proportions the same.

PREPARATION **20 MINUTES**
COOKING **25 TO 30 MINUTES**

Makes 24 bars
¾ cup (1½ sticks) unsalted butter, plus extra for greasing
½ cup superfine sugar
3 tablespoons dark corn syrup
2½ cups rolled oats
2 tablespoons all-purpose flour
a pinch of ground ginger
a pinch of salt
1 cup mixed dried fruit
⅓ cup mixture of pumpkin, sunflower, and sesame seeds

1 Preheat the oven to 375°F. Grease and line a shallow 12 x 14 inch baking pan or a pan that has sides that add up to the same measurements.
2 Melt the butter, sugar, and corn syrup together in a pan set over low heat. Mix together the oats, flour, ginger, and salt. Stir into the butter mixture, then add the dried fruit and seeds.
3 Turn the mixture into the prepared pan and bake in the oven for 25 to 30 minutes, until golden. Cut into squares in the pan while still warm. Store in an airtight container for up to 1 week.

Candy

The frivolity of making candy and chocolates always pleases me. It is food for sheer pleasure rather than an everyday necessity; their purpose is only to delight or reward. But, for me, most of the fun lies in making them, then wrapping in pretty boxes or vintage jars to give as presents. Having said that, candy making does take some concentration and meticulous preparation. When dealing with boiling sugar syrups for fudge or sugar candy, you must watch the thermometer like a hawk, while melting chocolate can easily seize if left unattended or stirred too vigorously. So take your time and enjoy the process and you'll be rewarded with bags of sweet joy.

Dark Chocolate Truffles (page 72)

Barley Sugar

Candy doesn't get any more old-fashioned than barley sugar—a lemon-flavored sugar syrup boiled to such a high temperature that it will be hard and brittle and a joy to eat when cooled.

PREPARATION **5 MINUTES**
COOKING **20 MINUTES**

Makes about 14½ ounces
oil, for greasing
2 ¼ cups granulated sugar
⅔ cup water
1 unwaxed lemon, zest and juice
¼ teaspoon cream of tartar

1 Generously oil the work surface or silicone sheet you will be pouring the molten sugar onto.
2 Put the sugar and water into a medium pan over low heat, stirring occasionally until the sugar has dissolved fully. Wash down any sugar crystals from the sides of the pan with a wet pastry brush. Meanwhile, pare the zest of the lemon in large pieces, without the white pith; squeeze and reserve the juice.
3 Add the lemon zest and cream of tartar to the syrup, raise the heat, and boil it to 240°F. Add the lemon juice and continue boiling until the syrup reaches the hard-crack stage, 310°F. Remove the pan from the heat, dip the base briefly in cold water, then pour the syrup out onto the prepared work surface.
4 Allow the syrup to cool a little until it stiffens at the edges and begins to form a skin. Use an oiled palette knife to lift one edge of the hardening puddle and fold it into the center. Fold over the opposite edge to cover the double layer, making a three-layered rectangle.
5 Working quickly, use oiled scissors to cut the barley sugar into narrow strips. Twist each into a curly stick and set aside on the oiled surface to harden completely.
6 Wrap each piece of barley sugar individually in waxed paper or cellophane and store in an airtight container.

Cardamom Fudge

The subtle flavoring of cardamom in this fudge makes it quite irresistible.

Makes about 1¾ pounds
½ cup (1 stick) salted butter, plus extra
   for greasing
3½ cups granulated sugar
¾ cup water
1 (13-ounce) can sweetened condensed
   milk
½ teaspoon ground cardamom seeds

1 Grease an 8 x 12 inch nonstick pan.
2 Slowly heat the sugar in a heavy pan with the water, milk, and butter until it is dissolved completely. Wash down any sugar crystals from the sides of the pan with a wet pastry brush.
3 Raise the heat, boil the syrup to the soft-ball stage (235°F on a confectionery or sugar thermometer), remove the pan from the heat, and dip the base in cold water.

4 Let the syrup rest for a minute or two, then, with a wooden spoon, stir in the cardamom. Continue stirring until the syrup starts to grain and stiffen, then pour into the prepared pan.
5 While warm, mark into squares, then cut into pieces when cooled. Store in an airtight container, separated by wax paper.

Dried Fruit Balls

Easy, quick, and full of flavor and goodness, serve as petit fours with coffee.

Makes about 20 balls

½ cup dried apricots

¾ cup mixed raisins, golden raisins, and currants

½ cup soft prunes, pitted

⅓ cup sweetened dried cranberries

½ cup shelled pistachios

finely grated zest of 1 unwaxed lemon

¼ teaspoon ground cinnamon

a pinch of ground cloves

up to 2 tablespoons each honey and ground almonds as needed

¾ cup granulated sugar

1 Work the apricots, raisin mixture, prunes, cranberries, and pistachios through the finest blade of a grinder into a bowl. You can blend in a blender or food processor, but be careful not to overwork the mixture to a purée.

2 Sprinkle over the lemon zest, cinnamon, and cloves. Mix well, adding a little honey if too dry, or a spoonful of ground almonds if too sticky.

3 Put the sugar in a shallow dish. Form small spoonfuls of the fruit mixture into balls by rolling them between your palms. Roll the balls in the sugar, then set in individual petit four paper cases. Decorate with dried fruit if you like. They can be eaten at once or stored for 1 week or more in an airtight container.

Dark Chocolate Truffles

Give these truffles a fascinating whiff of smoke by adding a splash of an Islay malt whisky, such as Laphroaig. Alternatively, you could infuse the cream with black cardamom pods, which have a very different flavor from the more familiar green cardamom—or both. Brandy or fruit liqueurs are other possible flavorings.

PREPARATION **10 MINUTES**

COOKING **15 MINUTES**

Makes about 24 truffles

⅓ **cup plus 2 tablespoons heavy cream**

6 whole black cardamom pods

8 ounces dark chocolate

1 tablespoon Islay whisky

1 teaspoon vanilla extract

alkalized unsweetened cocoa,
 for dusting

1 Heat the cream and cardamom pods in a small pan or microwave until hot but not boiling. Let infuse until lukewarm.
2 Break the chocolate into a large bowl and set it over a small pan of water that has just boiled and been taken off the heat. Let the chocolate warm slowly, stirring until it is fully melted. Alternatively, melt it in a microwave.
3 Strain the warm cream into the melted chocolate, stirring until smooth.
4 Let the mixture cool to room temperature before incorporating the whisky and vanilla and whisking the mixture until it lightens in color and holds soft peaks. Chill for 10 minutes to firm before forming the truffles.
5 Sift a thick layer of unsweetened cocoa onto a baking sheet. Cover another with wax paper. With 2

teaspoons, drop small, even-size blobs of the mixture into the cocoa. Dust your fingers with cocoa, roll each blob into a ball, roll it in the cocoa, and set it on the paper.
6 The truffles are ready to eat as they are, or can be rolled in chopped nuts or finely grated chocolate, or dipped in melted chocolate and decorated with gold leaf (see page 67 and Tip below).

Tip

For a bit of festive sparkle, use gold leaf for decoration (you'll need loose, not transfer gold—available on the Internet). Touch the thin gold sheets with a fine artist's brush—tiny pieces will stick to it and can be transferred to the truffles.

Candied Peel

PREPARATION **30 MINUTES PLUS STANDING**
COOKING **ABOUT 2 HOURS**

Makes about 1 pound 3 ounces
4 unwaxed oranges
4 cups water
3 ¼ cups granulated sugar

TO FINISH (OPTIONAL)
superfine sugar, for dredging
melted dark chocolate

Candied peel takes several days to prepare but the flavor is incomparable to the commercial variety and keeps for several months in an airtight container.

1 Cut the oranges into quarters and remove the flesh. Put the peel into a large pan with the water. Bring to a boil then simmer very gently for about 1 hour until the peel is tender but keeps its shape.

2 Reserve 2½ cups of the cooking liquid. Drain the peel and put in a nonmetallic bowl.

3 Dissolve 2¼ cups of the sugar in a pan with the reserved cooking liquid. When all the sugar is dissolved, turn up the heat and boil for 1 minute. Pour over the peel, cover, and let stand for 24 hours.

4 The next day, strain the liquid into a pan and add the remaining sugar. Dissolve and boil as in step 3. Pour over the peel, cover, and let stand for another 24 hours.

5 On day 3, put the peel and syrup into a heavy-bottom pan and bring to a boil. Simmer for 30 to 60 minutes until the pith is transparent—this will depend on the thickness of the peel. Transfer to a bowl, cover, and let the peel stand in the liquid for 4 days.

6 On day 7, drain and leave the peel on a wire rack in a cool, dry place for 1 week until no longer sticky.

7 To make a pleasing gift, the peel can be cut into slices and dusted with superfine sugar while still slightly tacky or the ends dipped into melted chocolate and left to set.

8 Layer the peel between sheets of wax paper. Alternatively, store in an airtight container for several months and use when needed in baking.

Dairy

The dairy products we take for granted today are often the result of happy accidents in the past—tweaked by generations of dairymaids and farmers' wives into constancy by experience and handed down. But, with a little technical help, you can achieve satisfying results in your own kitchen, too. The small but pleasurable miracles that convert fresh cream into golden butter and milk into soft, yielding cheese and tangy yogurt are as easily performed at home, albeit on a smaller scale, without taking away from the delights of their magical and delicious transformation.

Butter, Cream, and Yogurt

Generations ago, country cooks would make their own butter, clotted cream, and yogurt to use up surplus milk supplies that otherwise would have spoiled. Nowadays, of course, there is no incentive: supermarkets offer an abundance of these products, and surely it takes up too much time and would need hard-to-learn, long-forgotten domestic skills? The good news is that simple dairy products are easily achievable by the home cook and extremely satisfying to make.

Modern equipment such as stand mixers may not be as aesthetically pleasing as an old-fashioned butter churn but it takes away all the hard work, enabling butter to be created in a matter of minutes. Yogurt simply needs to be left in an airing cabinet overnight and clotted cream can be cooked on the kitchen stovetop. If you need any more encouragement, just imagine your own creamy butter and tangy yogurt served at breakfast or a dollop of clotted cream with scones and jam.

Dairy kitchenalia

There is a wealth of secondhand dairy items available that will make your finished butter look even more appealing. Butter pats, molds, and stamps as well as old-fashioned churns and dairy thermometers can be found on auction Web sites, in antiques stores, and, if you're lucky, at garage sales. Butter pats are quite common and you can pick up a reasonable pair for very little. Prices of molds depend on their size and rarity.

Butter

PREPARATION **10 MINUTES**

*Makes about 2½ cups butter and
2½ cups buttermilk*
5 cups heavy cream
¼ teaspoon salt (optional)

Making butter is very simple: heavy cream needs to be shaken or beaten to a point where the buttermilk and butterfat separate. This can be done in an old-fashioned churn, by shaking the cream vigorously in a jam jar (which takes at least 30 minutes), or by the easiest method, a stand mixer. If you use the latter, don't make my mistake and leave it unattended. I went out of the pantry to stir some frying onions in the kitchen. I heard a thud (the separation of butter and buttermilk), then a large splash as the buttermilk shot into the air covering the walls, counter, and floor!

1 Remove the cream from the fridge 1 to 2 hours before you want to make the butter so that it comes to room temperature.

2 Pour the cream into the bowl of a stand mixer with the K-beater (the whisk attachment used for heavy beating or whipping) attached. Beat on medium speed. Keep watch as it will suddenly separate into lumps of butter and a pool of buttermilk. Strain off the buttermilk into a jug and chill until needed. You can drink it or use it to make Buttermilk Scones (see page 80) and Whole Wheat Soda Bread (see page 18).

3 Put the lumps of butter into a colander and, with the cold tap running, gently squeeze and knead to remove excess buttermilk—gradually the liquid you squeeze out will run clear. You must do this or the butter will go rancid very quickly. Using butter pats will press out the liquid in the same way.

4 To make salted butter, add a scant ¼ teaspoon salt and knead in thoroughly. Taste—if it's too salty, you can rinse it out again with cold water.

5 Wrap in wax paper. Unsalted butter keeps for 2 to 3 days in the refrigerator; salted butter for up to 1 week; both can be frozen for up to 1 month.

Anchovy Butter

Herb Butter

Cinnamon Butter

Variations

Cinnamon Butter

Mash ½ cup (1 stick) butter with
1 tablespoon ground cinnamon and
1 tablespoon light brown sugar. Shape
into a log, wrap in wax paper, and chill or
freeze. Spread on toast or crumpets.

Herb Butter

Mash ½ cup (1 stick) butter with
2 tablespoons freshly chopped herbs,
such as parsley, mint, tarragon, or
chives. Shape into a log, wrap in wax
paper, and chill or freeze. Cut into
½-inch disks and melt on steaks, pork
and lamb chops, chicken, and fish.

Anchovy Butter

Mash ½ cup (1 stick) butter with
1 tablespoon freshly chopped parsley,
6 anchovy fillets, 1 finely chopped
shallot, and the juice of half a lemon.
Shape into a log, wrap in wax paper, and
chill or freeze. Cut into ½-inch disks and
melt on steaks, pork and lamb chops,
chicken, and fish.

Buttermilk Scones

Use the buttermilk left over from butter making (see page 78)—if you use commercial buttermilk you will need slightly more than ²/₃ cup.

1 Preheat the oven to 425°F.
2 Sift the flour, salt, and baking powder into a bowl. Rub in the butter until the mixture resembles breadcrumbs.
3 With a flat-bladed knife, mix in the buttermilk to make a soft but not too sticky dough.
4 Turn out onto a lightly floured work surface, knead very lightly and briefly to bring together, then pat into a circle about ¾-inch thick. Cut out rounds with a 2½-inch cutter and put, spaced apart, onto a lightly greased baking sheet. Brush with beaten egg or milk.
5 Bake in the oven for 12 to 15 minutes, until risen and golden. Let cool on a wire rack, then serve with jam and lots of homemade clotted cream (see page 81).

PREPARATION **15 MINUTES**
COOKING **12 TO 15 MINUTES**

Makes 6 to 8 scones
1²/₃ cups self-rising flour
a pinch of salt
1 teaspoon baking powder
3 tablespoons cold unsalted butter, diced, plus extra for greasing
½–²/₃ cup buttermilk
beaten egg or milk, to glaze

Clotted Cream

Traditionally, clotted cream was made from cream that was left to rise to the surface of the milk in the dairy, then "cooked" in large shallow pans until it formed a golden crust. Here I've made it with a carton of heavy cream.

PREPARATION **5 MINUTES PLUS COOLING**
COOKING **ABOUT 5 HOURS**

Makes ⅔–1 ¼ cups
1 ¼–2 ½ cups heavy cream, or however much you want to make

1 Put the cream into a double boiler or bain-marie set over the lowest heat. If you don't have a double boiler, put the cream into a heatproof bowl set inside a pan. Pour in enough hot water so that it comes halfway up the sides of the bowl. Let cook gently for about 5 hours undisturbed, until a golden crust forms on the surface. The cream must not bubble or boil.

2 Cover and let stand overnight in a cool place, then spoon off the clotted cream and transfer to the refrigerator until needed. The heavy cream left underneath can be used as usual in recipes.

Clotted Cream Fudge

Replace the vanilla extract with a few drops of coffee or almond extract for a change of flavor.

PREPARATION **15 MINUTES PLUS COOLING**
COOKING **30 MINUTES**

Makes about 1 ¼ pounds
1 ⅓ cups superfine sugar
⅓ cup dark corn syrup
1 cup clotted cream (see previous recipe)
½ teaspoon vanilla extract

1 Put all the ingredients except the vanilla into a heavy-bottom pan and set over low heat to dissolve the sugar. Lightly grease an 8-inch square pan.

2 Turn up the heat and boil the mixture until it reaches 212°F on a sugar thermometer. Turn the heat down to a steady boil until the temperature reaches 240°F—up to 20 minutes. Stir frequently to keep the mixture from catching on the base of the pan.

3 Carefully pour the fudge into a bowl, stir in the vanilla, and let stand until the temperature has dropped to 122°F. Beat vigorously until the fudge thickens and turns from glossy to matte. Turn into the pan and level with the back of a spoon. Let set and cut into squares when completely cooled.

Plain Yogurt

Save a little of your first batch to make your next. Straining it through a cheesecloth bag gives a Greek-style yogurt. It is also delicious drizzled with runny honey.

PREPARATION **10 MINUTES PLUS SETTING**

Makes about 3 cups
3 cups whole milk
2 tablespoons full-fat plain yogurt

1 Bring the milk to a boil in a pan set over medium heat. Take off the heat and let cool to about 110°F. Put the yogurt in a large ceramic or earthenware bowl.
2 When the milk has cooled to the correct temperature, remove and discard the skin and whisk the milk into the yogurt.
3 Put the ceramic bowl into another larger bowl and pour boiling water in between. Wrap the bowls in a large towel, covering the yogurt completely, and let stand in a warm place, ideally an airing closet, for at least 4 hours. The yogurt should set firm. If not, check again after an hour—the longer you leave it the thicker and sharper tasting it will be. Store in the refrigerator until needed, for up to 1 week.

Cucumber Yogurt Dip

Serve this fresh, tangy dip with strips of toasted whole-wheat pita bread or as an accompaniment to a spicy curry.

PREPARATION **15 MINUTES**

Makes about 1 cup
half a cucumber, seeded and diced
a pinch of ground cumin
1 tablespoon chopped fresh cilantro
1 tablespoon chopped fresh mint, plus extra to garnish
1 cup homemade plain yogurt (see opposite)
sea salt

1 Mix together all of the ingredients, reserving a spoonful of the cucumber, and season with sea salt to taste.
2 Serve in a small dish topped with the reserved cucumber and some chopped mint.

Scented Yogurt Cooler

Traditionally this type of drink tends to be rather sweet, so start off with half the amount of sugar, then tweak and add to suit your palate.

PREPARATION **10 MINUTES**

Makes about 1¾ cups or 2 glasses
1½ cups homemade plain yogurt (see opposite)
1 tablespoon orange flower water or rose water
3 tablespoons heavy cream
3–6 tablespoons superfine sugar, to taste
a handful of ice cubes

1 Put all of the ingredients into a blender or food processor and blend until combined.
2 Pour into tall glasses and serve the drink immediately.

Soft Cheeses

Country kitchens of old would turn their surplus milk supplies into pillowy mounds of fresh, mild cheese. The modern cook has no such need, yet it's a skill that's easy to master and brings much pleasure. Within hours and with little effort, cow's or goat's milk can be transformed into a refreshing soft cheese to be enjoyed on crusty bread, in a salad, or turned into a tangy cheesecake.

My grandmother made cheese with soured milk and a piece of cheesecloth. She'd hang the bundle by the back door, until the whey dripped away and a soft cheese could be unwrapped. You will also need rennet, a chemical found in calves' stomachs that will curdle milk and separate the curds, and whey for cheese making. Vegetarian rennet is available from good health food stores. Alternatively, lemon juice or vinegar will do a similar job.

Fresh Ricotta

This versatile fresh cheese can be used in a variety of sweet or savory recipes.

PREPARATION **10 MINUTES PLUS STANDING**
COOKING **5 MINUTES**

Makes about 2 cups
7 cups unhomogenized whole milk
3 tablespoons distilled white vinegar
 or 4 tablespoons lemon juice or a
 few drops of rennet
salt

1 Put the milk into a stainless steel saucepan and stir in the vinegar, lemon juice, or rennet.
2 Put the pan over very low heat and bring the milk up to a temperature of 203°F.
3 Remove from the heat and leave in a warm place—77–104°F—for about 6 hours, or until it separates into solid curds and liquid whey.

4 Line a sieve with cheesecloth and ladle in the curds and whey. Once drained you should be left with ricotta that has the consistency of thick yogurt. For a firmer ricotta, draw the cheesecloth into a bag and hang up over a bowl in a cool place to drain until the desired texture is reached. Add salt to taste and store in the refrigerator for up to 5 days. It is at its best eaten after 24 hours.

Baked Ricotta Cheesecake

For a change, use ginger cookies for the base and replace the lemon with the zest of a large orange or a couple of limes.

PREPARATION **25 MINUTES PLUS CHILLING**
COOKING **45 MINUTES**

Serves 6 to 8

1½ cups crushed oat cookies
4 tablespoons (½ stick) unsalted butter, melted
1 cup drained fresh homemade ricotta (see opposite)
3 large eggs
⅔ cup superfine sugar
¾ cup full-fat plain yogurt
finely grated zest of 2 large lemons
⅓ cup golden raisins

1 Preheat the oven to 325°F.
2 Mix together the cookies and butter and press into the base of a deep 8-inch cake pan. Chill for 30 minutes.
3 Beat together the remaining ingredients except the golden raisins until smooth. Stir in the golden raisins. Pour into the cake pan and bake in the oven for 45 minutes, or until lightly golden and just set.
4 Turn off the oven and leave the cheesecake inside to cool with the oven door ajar—this should keep the surface from cracking. Chill until ready to serve and consume within 3 days

Soft Goat Cheese

Don't throw away the whey as you can use it to replace water in breadmaking. Warm it gently until tepid before using. It freezes well until you need it, too.

PREPARATION **10 MINUTES PLUS SETTING**

Makes about 4½ cups
8 cups whole goat's milk
8 drops rennet, mixed with cooled boiled water
finely chopped herbs (optional)
salt (optional)

1 Heat the milk to 176°F, then stir in the rennet. Let cool for a few hours, until the milk is set.
2 Line a colander with sterilized cheesecloth. Cut the curd into cubes and gently spoon into the cheesecloth. Gather in the corners, tie with string, and hang over a bowl in a cool place for the whey to drain away. The longer you let it hang, the firmer it will become. For soft cheese, let stand for about 3 hours; for firm cheese about 6 hours.
3 Shape the cheese as you wish. For example, roll into a log shape, then roll in finely chopped herbs. Salting the cheese means it will keep, refrigerated, for up to 1 week.

Tip
You can also use the same method to make a basic soft cheese with whole cow's milk.

Goat Cheese Toasts

Serve these toasts as a starter for six or a light lunch for two.

PREPARATION **5 MINUTES**
COOKING **ABOUT 10 MINUTES**

Serves 6
6 slices French bread
1–2 tablespoons walnut oil
1 garlic clove, sliced in half lengthwise
½ cup homemade goat cheese (see above), formed into a log and cut into 1-inch slices
salad leaves, to serve

1 Preheat the oven to 350°F. Brush the bread on both sides with the oil and rub with the cut side of the garlic clove.
2 Arrange the bread on a baking sheet and bake in the oven for 5 minutes. Put a slice of cheese on top of each piece of bread and return to the oven for 5 to 7 minutes, until the cheese is soft but not melted. Serve with salad leaves.

A Simple Goat Cheese Salad

Try rolling the homemade goat cheese in dried chile flakes or crushed black or mixed peppercorns.

PREPARATION **15 MINUTES**
COOKING **10 MINUTES**

Serves 4

2 thick slices fresh country-style bread
1 tablespoon canola oil
1 cup homemade soft goat cheese (see opposite)
2 tablespoons chopped fresh mixed herbs (such as parsley, chives, and lemon thyme)
3 tablespoons hazelnut oil
1 tablespoon white wine vinegar
1 garlic clove, crushed
a squeeze of lemon juice
2 cups salad leaves
salt and freshly ground black pepper
¼ cup roughly chopped toasted hazelnuts
croutons, to serve

1 Preheat the oven to 400°F.

2 Cut the fresh country-style bread into cubes and toss in the canola oil. Spread out onto a baking sheet. Bake in the oven for 10 minutes, until golden and crisp. Set aside to cool.

3 Shape the soft goat cheese into a log, then roll in the chopped mixed herbs. Chill until firm.

4 Pour the hazelnut oil and white wine vinegar into a screw-top jar with the crushed garlic, lemon juice, and plenty of seasoning. Shake well to combine.

5 Just before serving, gently toss the salad leaves with the dressing. Divide among 4 plates, top with slices of goat cheese, and garnish with the toasted hazelnuts and croutons. Add a final flourish of freshly ground pepper.

Mascarpone

You can find tartaric acid in good pharmacies or from home-brewing Web sites.

PREPARATION **5 MINUTES PLUS CHILLING**
COOKING **ABOUT 10 MINUTES**

Makes about 1¾ cups
2½ cups heavy cream
a large pinch of tartaric acid
confectioners' sugar (optional)

1 Put the cream into a stainless steel pan and heat gently to 176°F. Add the tartaric acid and stir constantly for 10 minutes. Curds should form.
2 Line a colander with cheesecloth and spoon in the curds and whey. Let the whey drain away thoroughly.
3 Put the colander in a bowl in the refrigerator and let drain overnight. Sweeten with confectioners' sugar if you like.

Mascarpone Sauce for Pasta

Choose a pasta such as spaghetti or linguine so that the creamy sauce clings to the strands.

PREPARATION **5 MINUTES**
COOKING **ABOUT 10 MINUTES**

Serves 2
1½–2 cups pasta
3 tablespoons homemade mascarpone (see previous recipe)
2 egg yolks
½ cup grated Parmesan, plus extra to serve
a drizzle of olive oil
½ cup chopped prosciutto or bacon
a few chopped sage leaves
freshly ground black pepper

1 Cook the pasta according to the package instructions.
2 Meanwhile, mix together the mascarpone, yolks, and Parmesan. Heat the oil in a small pan and fry the prosciutto or bacon until golden.
3 Drain the pasta, reserving a few tablespoons of the cooking water. Return the pasta to the pan and toss with the mascarpone mixture and prosciutto or bacon. Stir in enough of the pasta water to make a creamy sauce.
4 Serve at once with the sage, plenty of Parmesan, and plenty of black pepper.

Serves 6

4 cups mixed soft summer berries

**4–5 tablespoons sweet dessert wine
 (such as Muscat de Beaumes
 de Venise)**

1 tablespoon confectioners' sugar

**1 cup homemade mascarpone
 (see opposite)**

1 cup heavy cream

a few drops vanilla extract

Fresh Mascarpone with Berries

Fresh mascarpone has a tangy yet creamy flavor that works especially well with soft summer berries in place of whipped heavy cream.

1 Put the mixed berries into a bowl with 2–3 tablespoons of the sweet dessert wine and let macerate for 1 hour for the fruit to release its juices.

2 Beat the remaining sweet dessert wine and the confectioners' sugar with the mascarpone until smooth.

3 In a separate bowl, whip the heavy cream to soft peaks with the vanilla. Gently fold into the mascarpone mixture.

4 Layer the mascarpone mixture and fruit in 6 serving glasses, finishing with a layer of fruit.

Ice Cream and Sherbet

Creamy or refreshing, rich or zesty, ice cream, sherbet, and granita add a welcome touch of luxury to the country cook's practical repertoire. Once a sign of wealth and privilege by those who could afford ice houses at sumptuous Victorian feasts, the advent of home freezers now makes the art accessible to all and no less irresistible. You will be rewarded with a deliciousness that belies the simplicity of the ingredients: the creamiest milk and freshest eggs combined with a touch of sugar and the freshest, ripest berries or darkest chocolate is all that's required for pure bliss.

Rich Vanilla Ice Cream
(page 96)

INGREDIENTS

Ice cream and sherbet are at their best when made from good-quality, simple ingredients. **Fruit** should be fresh and perfectly ripe, especially when making sherbet, as it will only be mixed with sugar syrup, so the flavor needs to shine through. Acid fruits, such as **citrus**, **berries**, and **passion fruit**, make particularly good sherbet. However, certain fruits like **pineapple** and **kiwi** contain an enzyme called bromelain that hinders or prevents successful freezing. Use **alcohol** sparingly—too much will also inhibit the freezing process and can make an ice cream taste harsh. White granulated and superfine **sugars** are preferable for crystal clear sugar syrups to add sweetness and hinder the formation of too many ice crystals; too much sugar, though, and the ice will remain slushy. Higher fat content **milk** and **cream** give a richer, smoother taste and also prevent too many ice crystals from forming; however, too much in proportion to other ingredients will make it dense and crumbly. **Crème fraîche** adds a pleasant sour note while **yogurt** retains its characteristic flavor and is lower in fat. A squeeze of **lemon juice** balances sweetness while a pinch of **salt** heightens flavors. **Nuts** and **chocolate chips** add pleasing texture and crunch and should be added when the ice cream has been churned. Adding **rosemary**, **mint**, or **basil** to sherbet creates an elegant palate cleanser.

EQUIPMENT

Electric **ice-cream makers** are desirable but not essential: excellent ice cream can be made with a hand **whisk**, a bit of elbow grease, and frequent attention (the still-freezing method). However, when making smooth sherbet and custard-based ice cream their constant churning does prevent ice crystals from forming in the mixture. The most expensive ice-cream makers have a built-in refrigeration unit that chills the mixture while it churns; cheaper models have removable containers that need to be put in the freezer for 24 hours before churning. The drawback with the latter is that they need to be frozen again before you can make more, whereas another batch of ice cream can be made immediately with the more sophisticated versions. Granita is the simplest ice to make: its coarse, granular texture is achieved by frequent stirring with a fork every 30 minutes during the freezing process to break up ice crystals. When making mousse and meringue-based parfaits, a

hand-held electric mixer for whisking cream, a **sugar thermometer**, and a **heavy-bottom saucepan** for making sugar syrups are also useful. Metal ice-cream **molds** can be used to create intricately shaped parfaits—look for them at antique fairs and scour junk stores. Otherwise, a **loaf pan** lined with **plastic wrap** is an adequate substitute.

A BIT OF TECHNIQUE

• If you don't have an ice-cream maker, you will need to use the still-freezing method. Put the mixture in a shallow freezerproof container and freeze for 2 hours, or until ice crystals form at the edges. Turn into a bowl and beat with a hand-held electric mixer. Pour back into the container and return to the freezer. Repeat every 2 hours until the ice cream or sherbet is completely frozen.

• It is possible to add extra smoothness to sherbet: when almost fully frozen, blend quickly with one egg white in a blender or food processor, then return to the freezer until solid.

• Before churning or still-freezing, fruit purees, sugar syrups, and custard bases should be completely cold.

• Always scald (bring to just below boiling point) milk before using in ice-cream bases—it will give a smoother mouthfeel to the finished ice cream.

• Custard bases benefit from standing in the refrigerator for up to 24 hours to develop their flavors.

• When making parfaits, never fill the mold to the top to allow room for expansion as it freezes; to unmold, dip the mold very briefly into hot water.

• Remember that the ice cream or sherbet mixture should be overly sweet or strong tasting because freezing mutes flavor.

• Removing from the freezer 30 minutes before serving will improve taste and texture.

• Do not refreeze ice cream once it has melted as it can contain potentially harmful bacteria that could cause food poisoning.

Top left: scalded milk is infused with a vanilla bean.
Top right: blending the freshest egg yolks with superfine sugar.
Bottom left: gently cooking the custard base until thickened; draw your finger across the wooden spoon to test if it is the right consistency.
Bottom right: whisking the partially frozen ice cream every 2 hours if making by hand.

Rich Vanilla Ice Cream

This ice cream is made with a custard base, which can be adapted and flavored with fruit purees, chocolate, or coffee. It keeps for up to 1 month in the freezer.

PREPARATION **40 MINUTES PLUS FREEZING**
COOKING **5 MINUTES**

Serves 4 to 6
1 vanilla bean
1¼ cups whole milk
4 egg yolks
⅔ cup superfine sugar
1¼ cups heavy cream

1 Split the vanilla bean lengthwise and scrape out the seeds. Put the bean and seeds in a saucepan with the milk over medium heat. Heat the milk until hot but not boiling, then take off the heat and let infuse for 30 minutes.
2 Mix together the egg yolks and sugar in a medium bowl. Remove and discard the vanilla bean and blend the milk into the yolk mixture using a wooden spoon or a whisk.
3 Rinse the milk saucepan and return the milk and egg mixture to the dry saucepan. Cook over medium-low heat, stirring constantly until the mixture has thickened enough to coat the back of a wooden spoon. Be careful not to overheat or the mixture will curdle.
4 Pass the mixture through a sieve into a chilled bowl. Transfer the bowl to the refrigerator to chill—this is your custard base (which you can go on to add other flavors to if you wish).
5 Stir in the cream, then churn in an electric ice-cream maker following the manufacturer's directions or transfer to a shallow freezerproof container, put in the freezer, and beat every 2 hours until the texture is creamy (see page 94).

Lavender and Honey Ice Cream

To make lavender sugar, bury the flowers from 2 sprigs of fresh or dried lavender into a large jar of superfine sugar. Let infuse for 2 weeks before using.

PREPARATION **40 MINUTES PLUS FREEZING**
COOKING **5 MINUTES**

Serves 4 to 6
1 recipe Rich Vanilla Ice Cream custard base (see previous recipe), made with ¾ cup lavender sugar (see above)
2 tablespoons lavender honey
1¼ cups heavy cream

1 Make the rich vanilla custard base as described in the previous recipe, replacing the superfine sugar with lavender sugar. If you cannot find lavender sugar, infuse the milk with 12 heads of lightly bruised lavender.
2 Stir in the honey and cream, then chill until cold. Churn in an electric ice-cream maker following the manufacturer's directions or transfer to a shallow freezerproof container, put in the freezer, and beat every 2 hours until the texture is creamy (see page 94).

Nutmeg and Bay Leaf Ice Cream

This subtle and delicate ice cream is particularly delicious served with warm apple pie.

PREPARATION **40 MINUTES PLUS FREEZING**
COOKING **5 MINUTES**

Serves 4 to 6
1 recipe Rich Vanilla Ice Cream custard base (see recipe on this page), made with 3 large bay leaves
1 teaspoon grated nutmeg
1¼ cups heavy cream

1 Make the rich vanilla custard base as described in the previous recipe, infusing the milk in step 1 with the bay leaves instead of the vanilla bean.
2 Stir in the nutmeg and cream and then chill until cold. Churn in an electric ice-cream maker following the manufacturer's directions or transfer to a shallow freezerproof container, put in the freezer, and beat every 2 hours until the texture is creamy (see page 94).

Nutmeg and Bay Leaf Ice Cream

Lavender and Honey Ice Cream

Rich Vanilla Ice Cream

Blackcurrant and Mint Ice Cream

Meringue-based ice cream doesn't need to be churned and works particularly well with tart-tasting fruits that balance the sweetness of the base mixture.

PREPARATION **30 MINUTES PLUS FREEZING**
COOKING **10 MINUTES**

Serves 4 to 6
a small handful of mint leaves
3 cups blackcurrants
1 cup water
2 tablespoons crème de cassis
1½ cups superfine sugar
2 egg whites
1¼ cups heavy cream
a squeeze of lemon juice

1 Roughly bruise the mint leaves in a mortar and pestle to release their oils and put in a saucepan with the blackcurrants and ⅓ cup plus 2 tablespoons of the water. Heat gently until the berries soften and release their juices, about 5 minutes.
2 Push the blackcurrants and mint through a sieve into a bowl to extract the juice. Add the casis and let cool.
3 Dampen 4–6 individual molds with water and line with plastic wrap that overlaps the edges. Alternatively, you can use a 2-pound loaf pan.
4 Dissolve the sugar in a saucepan with the remaining water over gentle heat. Bring to a boil, then simmer, without stirring, until it reaches 250°F—firm-ball stage (drop a teaspoon of syrup into a bowl of cold water; it should make a firm ball when brought together with your fingers) on a sugar thermometer.
5 Meanwhile, whisk the egg whites in a clean, dry bowl until they form stiff peaks. In a separate bowl, whisk the cream until it forms soft peaks.
6 Whisk the hot sugar syrup into the egg whites and continue whisking until the mixture is cooled.
7 Fold the blackcurrant puree into the meringue base along with a squeeze of lemon juice. Then fold in the whipped cream. Turn the mixture into the prepared molds or loaf pan. Smooth over the surface, fold the excess plastic wrap over the top, and freeze for 24 hours.
8 When ready to serve, turn out of the molds and remove the plastic wrap.

Raspberry Ripple Parfait

A mousse-based ice cream doesn't need to be churned and the flavors can be varied with other fruit purees. As an alternative to ripples, you can completely combine the mousse base and cream with the puree for a more amalgamated mixture. This parfait will keep in the freezer for up to 3 months.

PREPARATION **30 MINUTES PLUS FREEZING**
COOKING **5 MINUTES**

Serves 4 to 6
4 cups raspberries
1 cup confectioners' sugar, sifted
a squeeze of lemon juice
3 egg yolks
⅓ cup superfine sugar
⅔ cup water
1¼ cups heavy cream
1 teaspoon vanilla bean paste

1 Line a dampened 2-pound loaf pan with plastic wrap that overlaps the edges.
2 Puree the raspberries in a blender or food processor, then push through a sieve to remove the seeds. Stir in the confectioners' sugar and lemon juice.
3 Put the egg yolks in a heatproof bowl and whisk by hand or with a hand-held electric mixer until well beaten.
4 Put the superfine sugar in a saucepan with the water and dissolve over low heat. Bring to a boil, then simmer, without stirring, until it reaches 250°F—firm-ball stage (drop a teaspoon of syrup into a bowl of cold water; it should make a firm ball when brought together with your fingers) on a sugar thermometer.
5 Continue whisking the eggs while pouring on the hot sugar syrup in a steady stream. Continue whisking until the mixture is thick, mousselike, and forms a ribbon trail. Let cool.
6 Whisk the cream in a separate bowl with the vanilla bean paste until it just holds its shape—it should be about the same consistency as the egg mixture.
7 Fold the cream into the egg mixture. Swirl in the raspberry puree to make ripples, then carefully pour into the prepared loaf pan. Smooth over the surface, fold the excess plastic wrap over the top, and freeze for 24 hours.
8 When ready to serve, turn the parfait out of the pan, remove the plastic wrap, and cut into slices.

Coffee Granita

Eat the granita as soon it's ready—leave it too long in the freezer and the ice crystals will be hard and crunchy.

PREPARATION **35 MINUTES PLUS FREEZING**

Serves 4 to 6
¾ cup light brown sugar
1 ¼ cups hot strong coffee
⅔ cup coffee liqueur

1 Stir the sugar into the hot strong coffee and mix until dissolved. Let cool.
2 Stir in the liqueur. Pour into a shallow freezerproof container—the depth of the liquid should be no more than 1 inch, so divide between a few containers if necessary.
3 Freeze for 30 minutes, then remove from the freezer and scrape any frozen mixture into the center with a fork. Return to the freezer.
4 Repeat every 30 minutes, until completely frozen with a grainy texture. Serve immediately.

Mango and Passion Fruit Yogurt Ice

Using a full-fat yogurt produces a richer, smoother result; lower-fat versions produce a grainier texture.

PREPARATION **20 MINUTES PLUS FREEZING**
COOKING **2 MINUTES**

Serves 4 to 6
1 small ripe mango, peeled, pitted, and chopped
juice of 1 lemon
¾ cup plus 1 tablespoon superfine sugar
2 medium eggs, plus 1 egg yolk
4 passion fruits
2 cups Greek-style yogurt

1 Puree the chopped mango in a blender or food processor until smooth.
2 Put the pureed mango, lemon juice, sugar, whole eggs and egg yolk, and passion fruits in a saucepan and cook for 2 minutes, or until thickened. Push through a sieve into a bowl to remove any fibrous strands and seeds. Cover the surface with plastic wrap to keep a skin from forming and chill until it's cold.
3 Fold the Greek yogurt into the fruit mixture. For a smoother result, churn in an electric ice-cream maker following the manufacturer's directions, or transfer to a shallow freezerproof container and freeze without mixing if you prefer.

Mint Sherbet

Sherbets should be eaten within 2 to 3 days.

PREPARATION **15 MINUTES PLUS FREEZING**
COOKING **ABOUT 10 MINUTES**

Serves 4 to 6
2¼ cups granulated sugar
3 cups water
a large handful of mint leaves
grated zest and juice of 1 lime

1 Dissolve the sugar in a saucepan with the water over gentle heat. Bruise the mint leaves in a mortar and pestle and add to the saucepan along with the lime zest. Bring to a boil, then simmer for 5 minutes. Take off the heat and let infuse for 30 minutes. Add the lime juice and strain into a bowl. Chill until cold.
2 Churn in an electric ice-cream maker following the manufacturer's directions or transfer to a shallow freezerproof container, put in the freezer, and beat every 2 hours until the texture is smooth.

Preserving

For country cooks, turning a glut of fruit or vegetables into a stock of preserves to fill the pantry or larder is immensely satisfying. They're surprisingly cheap to make, too, especially if you take time to do a little hedgerow foraging for extra seasonal ingredients. Late summer and autumn are the traditional time for picking and preserving the garden's bumper crops of fruit and vegetables, but there is nearly always some suitable product to make the basis of a chutney, jam, jelly, or marmalade whatever the time of year.

Marmalade

Can days begin any better than with smells of toast and coffee curling up the stairs and a jar of homemade marmalade catching the morning sunlight? The word marmalade has evolved from the middle ages originating from the Portuguese word *marmelada,* which was their name for quince paste (a bit like the Membrillo paste that's served with manchego cheese today).

Marmalade originally had a paste-like consistency and was made from all types of fruit.

Eventually more sugar and the peel of citrus fruits were added during the eighteenth century to make the consistency we know today. Bitter oranges like the Seville orange were preferred for their flavor. Generally, marmalade differs from jam in that it tends to have a bitter flavor rather than sweet.

Marmalade was first fashionable as a part of the dessert course at banquets, and migrated to the breakfast table by way of the medicine chest and a reputation for curing colds.

From left to right:
Thick-cut Seville Orange Marmalade;
Three Fruit Marmalade (at back);
Clementine Marmalade (at front);
and Lemon and Honey Marmalade.

INGREDIENTS

New Year is the traditional time for marmalade making as it marks the short season of **Seville oranges**, which appear for a few weeks only in late January and February. Sevilles are spared the antifungal wax treatment given to other citrus fruits, so don't need such a ruthless scrubbing. But all manner of citrus varieties make marvelous marmalade. **Grapefruit** and **lemons** share a tantalizing bitterness with Sevilles, while sweet oranges and all the loose-skinned varieties such as **clementines**, **tangerines**, and **satsumas** have their own distinctive flavors. Sevilles, grapefruit, and lemons have lots of **pectin** and **acid**, the two ingredients that, when combined with sugar, ensure a well-set preserve. Sugar is the other essential ingredient, and there is a wide choice. The cheapest is white **granulated sugar**. **Less refined sugars** make good-looking marmalades if they are pale. **Dark, unrefined sugars** are useful for adding color and flavor but will be only a small proportion of the total amount used in any recipe. It is worth noting that British marmalade is traditionally not overly sweet but has a sharp, refreshing flavor.

EQUIPMENT

The kit required is fairly straightforward. A **preserving kettle**, wider at the rim than the base, is ideal because it encourages rapid evaporation and is large enough to allow the fast-boiling preserve to rise without boiling over. A sizable **Dutch oven** or **large pan** is a better substitute than a tall pasta boiler or stockpot. Add a clean **board**, a very **sharp knife**, a **lemon squeezer** or reamer, a **strainer**, some **cheesecloth** and **string**, **recycled jars**, **lids**, or **jam pot covers**, a **wooden spoon**, a couple of **bowls**, and a **ladle** and you are nearly there. The only specialized piece of equipment I would not be without is a **canning funnel**, which allows you to fill the hot jars with a minimum of sticky drips and dribbles.

MAKING CHIP MARMALADE

I like what is called chip marmalade, which has pieces of tender peel suspended in a richly flavored gel. This is what we'll be making. The second type, equally traditional, pulverizes whole cooked fruit and makes dense, opaque marmalade that is quick and simple to produce but not quite so good to eat or look at.

The essential thing with chip marmalade is to cook the peel until it is really tender—tender enough to squish between finger and thumb—before adding the sugar. When the sugar goes in, stir the mixure over low heat until every grain has melted before turning up the heat and boiling to setting point. Take your time. Leave an undissolved grain or two of sugar and your marmalade may crystallize in its pot as the sugar reverts.

JUDGING THE SETTING POINT

This requires attention and a little skill. Don't hurry. Prepare a stack of small plates by chilling them in the refrigerator. Bring the marmalade mixture to a rolling boil that cannot be stirred down. Let it boil for about 10 minutes, then start testing for a set. Take the pan off the heat and drop a teaspoonful of the marmalade on a chilled plate. Leave it for a minute and then push it with your finger. When the mixture thickens enough to wrinkle, it will set. If it stays runny, return the pan to a boil for a few more minutes, then test again. It should not need more than 20 minutes altogether. The variability depends on the fruit and how much evaporation has taken place while tenderizing the chips.

CANNING YOUR MARMALADE

When setting point is reached, take the pan off the heat, skim off any froth, and let the marmalade cool and thicken enough to hold its peel in suspension. Now ladle it into the warm, sterilized jars. If you are using wax paper disks and transparent jam pot covers, put on the wax disks now, cover the batch with a clean cloth, and let stand until completely cooled before applying the covers. If you are using lids, cover with a clean cloth until completely cooled before putting on the lids. Covering warm jars results in condensation, which encourages mold to form. If you are making different types of marmalade, label while you still remember which is which.

STERILIZING

To sterilize jars, lids, seals, and funnels, wash in hot, soapy water and put in an oven preheated to 300°F.

Top left: boil vigorously to bring the marmalade to setting point.
Top right: let the marmalade stand before canning.
Bottom left: testing for setting point.
Bottom right: can the marmalade while it is still hot.

Thick-Cut Seville Orange Marmalade

Adding a slug of whisky or cider brandy just before canning the marmalade adds flavor. Don't worry about consuming spirits at breakfast time—the heat of the marmalade evaporates the alcohol, leaving only extra flavor.

PREPARATION **40 MINUTES PLUS SOAKING**
COOKING **2½ HOURS**

Makes about 4 pounds
2 pounds Seville oranges
1 lemon
2 quarts water
10 cups granulated sugar
1 cup dark brown sugar
5 tablespoons whisky or cider brandy

1 Wash and dry the fruit, and cut in halves or quarters.
2 Set a strainer over a bowl and line it with a large double layer of cheesecloth.
3 Working over the strainer, juice the fruit, scouring the shells as you go, and dropping the seeds, squeezed flesh, and membranes into the cloth. A reamer is usually the easiest way to empty oranges and lemons cleanly. Reserve the juice squeezed from the fruit.
4 Tie all the residue into a loose bag and put it in a preserving pan with the water.
5 Shred the skins as finely as you like and add to the pan. Let soak for several hours or, better still, overnight.
6 Bring to a boil, reduce the heat, and let simmer, uncovered, until the peel is meltingly tender and the liquid has reduced by half—usually about 2 hours, but sometimes more. Cover the pan if too much evaporation is occurring before the peel is tender.
7 Remove the bag of seeds and bits and squeeze the liquid out of it back into the pan. Discard the contents of the bag. Add the sugar to the pan, plus the reserved juices.
8 Bring slowly to a boil, stirring until the sugar has dissolved completely. Raise the heat and boil hard until the setting point (see page 106) is reached, usually about 10 minutes. Let cool and thicken a little, then stir to redistribute the peel. Add the whisky and stir in before canning.

Variations

Lemon and Honey Marmalade

The inspiration for this marmalade is everyone's favorite cold cure. Choose a strongly flavored honey—you are using only a small amount in relation to the quantity of fruit—and cut the peel in short, stubby lengths.

PREPARATION **40 MINUTES PLUS SOAKING**
COOKING **2½ HOURS**

Makes about 5 pounds
2 pounds unwaxed lemons
13 cups water
10 cups granulated sugar
1¼ cups fragrant runny honey

Follow the recipe above for Thick-Cut Seville Orange Marmalade. Add the honey to the pan in step 7 with the sugar and reserved juices.

Three Fruit Marmalade

Choose citrus fruit that are heavy for their size to ensure maximum juiciness.

PREPARATION **40 MINUTES PLUS SOAKING**
COOKING **2½ HOURS**

Makes about 3 pounds
1 grapefruit
2 oranges
2 lemons
2 quarts water
10 cups granulated sugar

Follow the recipe above for Thick-Cut Seville Orange Marmalade. In step 3, in the case of grapefruit it is easier to quarter them, use a teaspoon inserted between the skin and the flesh to pick up a strip of membrane large enough to grip, then use your fingers to tear out the interior of the fruit, leaving a tidy shell (instead of using a reamer).

Pink Grapefruit Marmalade

Thick-Cut Seville Orange Marmalade

Clementine Marmalade (page 110)

Lemon and Honey Marmalade

Pink Grapefruit Marmalade

Grapefruit has a distinctive bitter edge very similar to Seville oranges, which makes it the best substitute for Sevilles when they are unavailable or out of season.

PREPARATION **40 MINUTES PLUS SOAKING**
COOKING **2½ HOURS**

Makes about 5 pounds
2 pounds pink grapefruit, about
 4 medium
10 cups water
1 ¼ cups granulated sugar
½ cup freshly squeezed lemon juice

Follow the recipe opposite for Thick-Cut Seville Orange Marmalade. In step 3, in the case of grapefruit it is easier to quarter them, use a teaspoon inserted between the skin and the flesh to pick up a strip of membrane large enough to grip, then use your fingers to tear out the interior of the fruit, leaving a tidy shell (instead of using a reamer). Also, in step 7, add the lemon juice at the same time as the sugar and reserved juices.

Clementine Marmalade

Tangerines, mandarins, and other similar loose-skinned citrus in season can be substituted for clementines. The generous quantity of lemon juice in this recipe helps to overcome the lack of pectin in these sweet citrus varieties. Finely sliced peel suits this recipe.

PREPARATION **40 MINUTES PLUS SOAKING**
COOKING **2½ HOURS**

Makes about 2 pounds
1 pound clementines
2 cups apple juice
2 cups water
3¾ cups granulated sugar
6 tablespoons freshly squeezed lemon juice

1 Wash and dry the fruit, and cut in halves or quarters.
2 Set a strainer over a bowl and line it with a large double layer of cheesecloth.
3 Working over the strainer, juice the fruit, scouring the shells as you go, and dropping the seeds, squeezed flesh, and membranes into the cloth. In the case of loose-skinned citrus such as clementines it is easier to quarter them, use a teaspoon inserted between the skin and the flesh to pick up a strip of membrane large enough to grip, then use your fingers to tear out the interior of the fruit, leaving a tidy shell.
4 Reserve the juice squeezed from the fruit.
5 Tie all the residue into a loose bag and put it in a preserving pan with the apple juice and water.
6 Shred the skins as finely as you like and add the peel to the pan. Let soak for several hours or, better still, overnight.
7 Bring to a boil, reduce the heat, and simmer, uncovered, until the peel is meltingly tender and the liquid has reduced by half—usually about 2 hours, but sometimes more. Cover the pan if too much evaporation is occurring before the peel is tender.
8 Remove the bag of seeds and bits and squeeze the liquid out of it back into the pan. Discard the contents of the bag. Add the sugar to the pan, plus the reserved juice and lemon juice.
9 Bring slowly to a boil, stirring until the sugar has dissolved completely. Raise the heat and boil hard until the setting point (see page 106) is reached, usually about 10 minutes. Let cool and thicken a little, then stir to redistribute the peel before canning.

Marmalade Muffins

Clementine marmalade makes a particularly good filling for these springy muffins, but any citrus flavor works well.

PREPARATION **30 MINUTES**
COOKING **20–25 MINUTES**

Makes about 12 muffins
1⅛ cups superfine sugar
7 tablespoons unsalted butter, softened
2 medium eggs
1 teaspoon baking soda
1 cup buttermilk (see page 78)
1¼ cups all-purpose flour
½ teaspoon salt
finely grated zest of 1 orange
¼ cup marmalade

1 Preheat the oven to 400°F, and line a 12-hole muffin pan with paper cases.
2 Cream the sugar and butter until light and fluffy. Beat in the eggs, one at a time.
3 Stir the baking soda into the buttermilk.
4 Sift together the flour and salt and fold into the creamed butter mixture with alternate spoonfuls of the buttermilk. Finally stir in the orange zest.
5 Divide half of the mixture between the 12 muffin cases. Put a teaspoonful of marmalade in the center of each one and top with the remaining mixture.
6 Bake in the oven for 20 to 25 minutes, until well risen and springy to the touch. The jammy centers will be very hot, so let the muffins cool a little before tasting them.

Jams and Jellies

For country cooks, it is a satisfying time of year when the gluts of summer and autumn can be turned into delicious jams and jellies. Wild plums, blackberries, and crab apples are all suitable for preserving while garden orchards are laden with a surplus of plums, pears, and quinces. If you don't have any fruit trees, visit a u-pick farm—it's far cheaper than the supermarket and supports local farmers. Then retreat to the kitchen, switch on the radio, and spend a rewarding afternoon chopping, simmering, and canning the fruits of your pickings. The result will be a pleasing stock of jewel-like preserves to cheer up the breakfast table and give your home-baked cakes a makeover.

INGREDIENTS

There's little you need in the way of specific ingredients to create jams and jellies. **Granulated sugar** is sufficient to produce a good set for most fruit. Choose firm, slightly underripe, unblemished **fruits**—overripe fruit contains less pectin. Fruit high in pectin, such as **apples, plums, damsons**, and **gooseberries**, will need little help with setting. **Blueberries, apricots**, and **raspberries** contain medium levels, while **strawberries, cherries, peaches**, and **rhubarb** contain the lowest amounts.

Adding **lemon juice** will boost pectin levels. **Liquid pectin** is also available. To make your own liquid pectin, put 9 pounds roughly chopped cooking apples (cores, peel, seeds, and all) in a large pan with enough water to just cover. Bring to a boil, then simmer for 20 minutes. Pour into a jelly bag and let drip overnight. Pour the liquid into a clean pan and boil until reduced by half. Freeze in batches: ⅔ cup will set about 2 pounds low-pectin fruit.

Stronger-flavored **redcurrants, blackcurrants, quince, blackberries, wild plums**, and **elderberries** are most suitable for making jellies and tend to be combined with blander apples, which are higher in pectin, to ensure a good set. **Quinces** are also high in pectin.

EQUIPMENT

It's worth investing in a **preserving kettle** because it will last a lifetime—they're wider at the top than the bottom, helping evaporation and allowing a fast-boiling preserve to rise without boiling over. Stainless steel is a good all-rounder or choose copper, although it's not suitable for making pickles and chutneys. A **thermometer** is useful rather than essential as you can test for a set with a chilled plate (see the technique section). **Jelly bag** kits are available from cookware stores or you can make your own: take two or three layers of scalded cheesecloth, tie each corner to the leg of an upturned stool, and put a bowl underneath. Buy pristine **jars** and **lids** and **waxed disks** from good cookshops or mail-order companies; old jars and lids can be used again once sterilized. A wide-mouth **canning funnel** will keep you from making a sticky mess while canning. Vintage-style labels are a pleasing touch, especially if you are planning to give the preserves as gifts, or make your own using luggage labels, stamp sets, and string.

A BIT OF TECHNIQUE

• Precook fruit in simmering water to soften the flesh and skin and encourage it to release pectin. Add just a splash of water to juicy fruits such as blackberries and currants; hard fruits including apples and quince should be almost covered.
• Warm the sugar in a heatproof bowl in a low oven—this helps it to dissolve more quickly when added to the fruit.
• To see if it has set, pop a few plates in the freezer to chill, drop a teaspoonful of the jelly or jam onto the plate, and let stand for a minute. Push with your finger—if it wrinkles it's set. If it doesn't, keep on boiling and retesting every couple of minutes.
• Jam containing pieces of fruit should stand for 15 minutes before canning to keep them from floating to the top of the jar; as a rule, jellies should be canned immediately unless extra ingredients are added. Seal immediately, then label the jars when completely cooled.
• To sterilize jars, lids, seals, and funnels, see the information on page 106.

jelly bag

canning funnel

Lavender and Lemon Jelly

Jellies are a little more versatile than jams: spread them on toast or scones or melt into savory sauces. Can this jelly in smaller jars for serving with roast lamb, so that it can be used up in one sitting.

PREPARATION **15 MINUTES PLUS STANDING**
COOKING **1 HOUR**

Makes about 3½ pounds
3½ pounds crab apples or baking apples
pared zest and juice of 2 large lemons
3 tablespoons lavender flowers
7 cups water
warmed sugar (see Tip below)

1 Roughly chop the apples, peel, core, and all—it contains valuable pectin. Put the fruit, lemon zest, juice, and 2 tablespoons of the lavender flowers into a large pan with the water. Cover and let simmer for 40 to 50 minutes, until tender.
2 Transfer the mixture to a jelly bag and let drip into a bowl for at least 4 hours or preferably overnight (use within 24 hours as the pectin levels will decrease). Don't be tempted to touch or squeeze the bag as it will cloud the final jelly—be patient and let it drip slowly.
3 Measure the juice, allowing 2 cups sugar for every 2½ cups of juice. Next, bring the juice to a boil in a preserving pan, then add the sugar to dissolve over low heat.
4 Boil rapidly for about 10 minutes (too long and the jelly will be rubbery). A couple of minutes before you reach the setting point (usually at about 8 minutes), turn down the heat to a bubbling boil. A rapid boil will trap lots of air bubbles and spoil the clarity of your jelly. Skim away any scum from the top.
5 Let stand for 15 to 20 minutes, until the jelly has thickened slightly. Stir in the remaining lavender—do this too soon and the flowers will float to the top of the jars. Carefully pour the jelly down the inside of the jar to minimize air bubbles. Seal the jars and let stand where they are until cooled to keep wrinkles from forming. Label your jars.

Tip
Sugar will melt more quickly if it is warm when added to liquid. Put the sugar in a heatproof bowl and place in the oven at its lowest setting for about 20 minutes, until warm but not hot.

Blackberry and Apple Jam

A traditional combination of ingredients, with flavor coming from the fragrant berries. Throwing in a few underripe berries will help with setting.

PREPARATION **15 MINUTES**
COOKING **35 MINUTES**

Makes about 3½ pounds
2½ pounds blackberries
juice of 2 lemons
1¾ cups water
1 pound 5 ounces crab apples or baking apples, peeled, cored, and roughly chopped
warmed sugar (see Tip, previous recipe)

1 Pick over the blackberries, rinse, and then put in a large pan with the juice of 1 lemon and ⅓ cup of the water. Cover and simmer for 10 to 15 minutes, until they are soft.

2 Put the apples in a separate pan with the remaining lemon juice and water. Cover and let simmer until soft and pulpy.

3 Blend the blackberries briefly in a blender or food processor, then push through a strainer to remove the seeds. You can skip this stage, but most people prefer a seed-free jam.

4 Measure the blackberry puree and apple pulp and put into a preserving pan with the same quantity of sugar. Slowly dissolve the sugar over low heat, then bring to a rapid boil for 10 to 20 minutes, until the setting point is reached—stir from time to time to make sure the fruit isn't catching on the bottom of the pan and adjust the heat if the jam is boiling too vigorously.

5 Once the setting point is reached, skim off the scum. Don't throw this away—it's edible, a cook's perk (eat it on toast)! Pour the mixture while still hot into hot sterilized jars or when completely cooled into cold jars—never can while just warm as this could make your jam go moldy. Seal, then label when completely cooled.

Wild Plum Jelly

This is traditionally made with sloes—a wild European plum. As a substitute, look for small dark, tart-flavored plums at the farmers' market or grow them in your garden.

PREPARATION **15 MINUTES**
COOKING **1 HOUR**

Makes about 3½ pounds
2 pounds wild plums
4 pounds crab apples or baking apples, roughly chopped
grated zest and juice of 1 lemon
warmed sugar (see page 116)

1 Put the wild plums in a pan with just enough water to cover. Let simmer for about 30 minutes, until soft and pulpy.
2 Simmer the apples, lemon zest, and juice in another pan with almost enough water to cover for 40 to 50 minutes.
3 Strain the fruit in a jelly bag.
4 Measure the juice, allowing 2¼ cups sugar per 2½ cups of juice. Bring the juice to a boil and then dissolve the sugar over low heat.
5 Boil rapidly until the setting point is reached—see Lavender and Lemon Jelly (page 116). Pot immediately and seal.

Plum Jam

Plums have a brief season—make them last a little longer by making a batch of this jam to perk you up during the winter months.

PREPARATION **15 MINUTES**
COOKING **50 MINUTES**

Makes about 3 pounds
3 pounds plums, halved and pitted
1¼ cups water
3 pounds warmed sugar (see page 116)

1 Put the plums into a preserving kettle with the water. Let simmer for 20 to 30 minutes, until the skins are soft.
2 Add the sugar, dissolve, then boil rapidly until the setting point is reached. Skim away the scum and any bits of skin that have loosened from the plums and can (see page 117).

Peach and Pear Jam

Peaches and pears are relatively low in pectin, so the high-pectin lemon juice gives them a helping hand to set.

PREPARATION **15 MINUTES**
COOKING **50 MINUTES**

Makes about 4½ pounds
2 pounds peaches or nectarines, peeled, pitted, and roughly chopped
2 pounds pears, slightly underripe, peeled, cored, and roughly chopped
½ cup water
grated zest and juice of 4 lemons
10 cups warmed sugar (see page 116)

1 Put the fruit in a preserving kettle with the water and the lemon zest and juice. Simmer for 20 to 30 minutes, until the fruit is tender but not mushy.
2 Add the sugar and dissolve over low heat. Boil rapidly until the setting point is reached. Let stand; can (see page 117).

Rose-Petal Jelly

This is an exquisitely colored jelly with the scent and taste of rose petals.

PREPARATION **20 MINUTES**
COOKING TIME **1 HOUR**

Makes about 3½ pounds
3½ pounds crab apples or baking apples, roughly chopped
pared zest and juice of 2 large lemons
6 cups scented rose petals
8½ cups water
warmed sugar (see page 116)
1–2 tablespoons rose water (optional)

1 Simmer the apples as for the Lavender and Lemon Jelly recipe (see page 116), minus the lavender, then strain.
2 Remove the white heels from the petals; roughly chop. Put into a small pan with 1¼ cups of the water and 2 teaspoons sugar. Let simmer for 10 minutes, then strain through a cheesecloth-lined strainer.
3 Measure the combined juice and continue from step 3 of the Lavender and Lemon Jelly recipe. Carefully taste the jelly—if the flavor is not pronounced enough, stir in a tablespoon or two of rose water. Pour into jars and seal.

Bakewell Pudding

Bakewell pudding is traditionally filled with raspberry jam, but this version uses Plum Jam (see page 118), which has a natural affinity with almonds.

PREPARATION **20 MINUTES PLUS CHILLING**
COOKING **30–35 MINUTES**

Serves 6 to 8

1 recipe Basic Flaky Pie Dough
  (see page 28)
2 tablespoons Plum Jam (see page 118)
½ cup candied citrus peel
3 large eggs
⅓ cup superfine sugar
½ cup (1 stick) unsalted butter, melted
1 teaspoon vanilla extract
½ cup ground almonds
thick heavy cream, to serve

1 Preheat the oven to 400°F. Roll out the pie dough on a lightly floured work surface to a thickness of ⅛ inch. Use it to line an 8-inch, 2-inch deep oval pie dish with a ¾-inch rim and crimp the edges with a fork. Chill for 30 minutes.
2 Spread the jam over the base of the pie dough shell and scatter with the candied citrus peel.
3 Whisk the eggs and sugar together until fluffy and lighter in color. Whisk in the butter and vanilla and fold in the ground almonds.
4 Pour the mixture into the pie dough shell and bake in the oven for 10 minutes. Turn down the oven temperature to 350°F and bake for another 20 to 25 minutes, until golden. Serve with thick heavy cream.

Chutney

Chutneys are the easiest preserves to make and one of the most rewarding. They provide instant gratification and a pantry full of treasures that only get better with time. We make them in high summer and early autumn because that's when gardens produce bumper crops. But there is nearly always some produce in season to make the basis of a chutney. There is a lot to be said for making a little, often, to furnish your shelves with a variety of relishes. After all, the whole point of chutneys is to charm the taste buds with spicy, sweet and sour bursts of flavor that flatter the hard cheeses, cold meats, pies, and curries that have come to seem naked without them.

Well-made chutney will keep for several years and improve rather than deteriorate provided that it is well sealed and not exposed to light. But the idea that chutney has to age for several months before eating stems, I think, from the days before cider and wine vinegars became common enough to take over from harsher malt vinegar. This leaves only the question of whether to make chutney that is mild and mellow or buzzing with heat and spice. No need to choose. Let's make both.

Chutney Shelf Life

Chutneys must be left for at least a month to age before eating—even slightly longer if you can bear the wait. During that time the vinegar will mellow and the spices will mingle and soften with the fruit and sugar. Store in a cool, dark place and they will keep for a year or two unopened and for about six months in the refrigerator once opened.

INGREDIENTS

Chutneys are made with **fruit and vegetables** preserved with vinegar, sugar, salt, and spices in infinitely variable combinations. In fact, even using the same recipe, it is not easy to get exactly the same result every time. They are wonderfully versatile users-up of almost any fresh fruit, whether ripe or unripe, and many vegetables, especially overgrown **zucchini**. The only proviso is that the produce used should be in good condition, so while it is fine to use **windfall** fruit such as **apples** or **plums**, it is important to discard all parts that are bruised, damaged, or moldy. **Dried fruits** are also traditional in chutneys, adding sweetness and concentrated depth of flavor in the case of **apricots**, **raisins**, **prunes**, **figs**, and **dried cranberries** or **cherries**.

Dark sugars such as raw brown and dark brown add color as well as sweetness. Use refined or paler unrefined varieties to accentuate the flavor and color of fruits such as plums, peaches, or dessert apples.

Inexpensive **malt vinegar** gets the job done. But good-quality **wine** and **cider vinegars** do it even better, producing chutneys that don't need long maturing to be agreeably mellow.

Heat comes from chiles and ginger. In old recipes these **spices** are invariably dried, but both are now readily available in fresh form to give good flavor as well as heat. Most other spices are used dried and work best when bruised and tied loosely in a cheesecloth bag, which is removed from the cooked chutney before it is canned. **Fennel** and **onion seeds** are an exception to this procedure and can be added directly to the chutney without grinding.

EQUIPMENT

A large capacity, wide-mouth **pan** made of a material that does not react with the acetic acid of vinegar is an absolute requirement. Brass or copper preserving pans are not suitable (the acetic acid in the vinegar will make the chutney taste bitter and will corrode the metal over time). Although a **stainless steel preserving kettle** is the ideal, I use an 11-inch round **casserole** with a vitreous enamel lining for making chutneys. Its thick base helps to prevent sticking. A **heat-diffuser** has the same effect when cooking on a gas burner. A **scale** for measuring ingredients, small squares of **cheesecloth** for wrapping spices, and a **long-handled wooden spoon** to stir the chutney with are all the equipment needed. This is a low-tech pastime.

New or recycled **jars** for bottling chutney can be almost any size or shape. The most important thing is to achieve a good seal with **lids** that do not react with vinegar as bare metal does, or allow evaporation as transparent jam pot covers do. Le Parfait-style glass canning jars with glass lids and rubber seals work perfectly, as do new lids with a nonreactive coating for screw-top jars. A **canning funnel** makes for easy mess-free bottling—remember to **label** your efforts. Most chutneys look, well, brown, no matter how distinctive their flavors.

A BIT OF TECHNIQUE

- Haste is the enemy of a good chutney. Chopping fruit and vegetables by hand is more time-consuming than using a grinder or food processor, but the finished chutney rewards the effort in both appearance and texture.
- Undercooking can result in poor texture and flavor.
- Chutney should be jammy in texture and the flavors well-blended in a whole that is more than the sum of its parts. When you think your chutney is ready, draw your wooden spoon across the base of the pan—it should leave a clear channel for the count of three.
- Chutney making is a fertile field for creative experiment. When I have ripe, well-flavored fruit to work with—say plums, a basket of peaches, or distinctively flavored dessert apples such as red delicious or McIntosh—I turn them into mild chutneys that let the taste of the fruit shine in its own right. Then I let rip with the chiles and spices when the chutney is based on unripe fruit or bland vegetables such as squash. Chutneys are pretty obliging, though, so don't be too fussed if the correct ingredients aren't on hand or you don't have quite enough of one thing: dried fruits, sugars, spices, and vinegar are interchangeable and the end result will still taste delicious. Besides, no chutney will taste exactly the same each time, which is part of its charm.
- To sterilize jars, lids, seals, and funnels, see the information on page 106.

Green Tomato Chutney

This is lovely with curries and cold meats. I like to assemble all the ingredients in the pan and let it stand overnight before starting to cook the chutney the next morning. This allows the sugar and salt to draw juices from the fruit and onions with the result that the pieces keep their shape when cooked and, while fully tender, don't disintegrate into a mush.

PREPARATION **45 MINUTES**

COOKING **ABOUT 2 TO 3 HOURS**

Makes 8 cups
2½ pounds green tomatoes
1 pound apples, baking or eating
1½ pounds onions
2 fresh red chiles, medium or hot
3 garlic cloves, peeled
1½-inch piece of fresh ginger, peeled
 and roughly chopped
3 cups white wine vinegar
5 cups granulated sugar
1 tablespoon salt

1 Chop the tomatoes, discarding any hard core pieces. Peel, core, and chop the apples into pieces of roughly the same size. Peel and chop the onions likewise. Put them all into a large nonreactive pan.
2 Halve the chiles and discard the stalks and seeds. Put them in a blender or food processor with the garlic, ginger, and a splash of the vinegar. Blend to a loose, smoothish paste and add it to the pan.
3 Add the rest of the vinegar, the sugar, and the salt. Put the pan over medium heat and stir frequently until the sugar has dissolved completely. Then cook the mixture down slowly, stirring more frequently as it thickens. When it is well cooked (about 2 to 3 hours), pour into sterilized jars and seal.

Red Tomato and Onion Seed Chutney

This sweet, mild, and mellow chutney is lovely with well-flavored curries, cold cuts of meats, and bread and cheese.

PREPARATION **45 MINUTES**

COOKING **ABOUT 2 TO 3 HOURS**

Makes 8 cups
2½ pounds ripe red tomatoes
1 pound apples, baking or eating
1½ pounds red onions
1 fresh red chile, medium or hot
1 large garlic clove, peeled
¾-inch piece of fresh ginger, peeled and roughly chopped
3 cups white wine vinegar
5 cups granulated sugar
1 tablespoon salt
2 tablespoons onion seeds

1 Chop the tomatoes, discarding any hard core pieces. Peel, core, and chop the apples into pieces of roughly the same size. Peel and chop the onions likewise. Put them all into a large nonreactive pan.
2 Halve the chile and discard the stalk and seeds. Put in a blender or food processor with the garlic, ginger, and a splash of the vinegar. Blend to a loose, smoothish paste and add it to the large pan.
3 Add the rest of the vinegar, the sugar, and the salt. Put the pan over medium heat and stir frequently until the sugar has dissolved completely. Add the onion seeds, then cook the mixture down slowly, stirring more frequently as it thickens. When it is well cooked (about 2 to 3 hours), pour into sterilized jars and seal.

Red Tomato and OnionSeed Chutney

Red Onion Marmalade

Onion marmalade has a made-in-heaven affinity with creamy blue cheeses and with cold cooked game, poultry, pâtés, and terrines. This version of what has become a very popular preserve is mellow and subtle and I can never make enough of it. Be sure the onions are cooked to a silky soft texture before adding the wine and vinegar.

PREPARATION **30 MINUTES**

COOKING **1 HOUR 20 MINUTES**

Makes about 3 cups
3 tablespoons light olive oil
1 pound 7 ounces red onions, very
   thinly sliced
1 teaspoon salt
1 teaspoon freshly ground black pepper
¾ cup superfine sugar
⅔ cup sherry vinegar
1 cup plus 2 tablespoons full-bodied red
   wine
2 tablespoons fresh raw beet juice or
   grenadine

1 Heat the oil in a heavy medium pan. Add the onions, salt, pepper, and sugar and stir. Cover and cook over low heat until the mixture has produced some liquid. Uncover and cook over gentle heat, stirring from time to time, for about 30 minutes, until the onions are soft. Don't allow them to brown.
2 Add the vinegar, wine, and beet juice or grenadine and continue to cook over slightly higher heat for about 30 minutes, until thickened a little.
3 Remove from the heat and pour at once into warm sterilized jars. Cool completely before sealing.

Variation

• Add 1 tablespoon fennel seeds with the liquid ingredients.

Pear and Pumpkin Chutney

Pears can be hard, ripe, or best of all a mixture of both, including windfalls if you have them. Any firm fleshed squash variety can be used. Butternut and acorn have good sweet flavors.

PREPARATION **50 MINUTES**

COOKING **ABOUT 2 TO 3 HOURS**

Makes about 8 cups
2 pounds pears, peeled, cored, and diced
3 cups pumpkin or butternut squash,
   peeled, seeded, and diced
3 cups roughly chopped onions
3 cups raisins, chopped if large
2 garlic cloves, peeled
2-inch piece of fresh ginger, peeled and
   roughly chopped
3 cups cider vinegar
2½ cups light brown sugar
1½ teaspoons salt
1 tablespoon black peppercorns
1 tablespoon allspice

1 Put the chopped pears, squash, onions, and raisins into a large nonreactive pan.
2 In a blender or food processor, blend the garlic, ginger, and a splash of the vinegar. Blend to a loose, smoothish paste and add it to the pan. Add the rest of the vinegar, the sugar, and salt.
3 Bruise the peppercorns and allspice with a mortar and pestle, and tie them loosely in cheesecloth.
4 Put the pan over low to medium heat and stir frequently until the sugar has dissolved completely and some liquid has been drawn from the fruit and vegetables. Add the spice bag and cook the mixture down slowly, stirring more frequently as it thickens.
5 When it is well cooked (about 2 to 3 hours), remove the spice bag and spoon the chutney into sterilized jars and seal.

Variations

• **Spicy Pear and Pumpkin Chutney**: to add a punch of heat to the chutney, include 2 to 3 medium to hot fresh chiles, seeded and roughly chopped in the blender mix of garlic and ginger. Alternatively, add chile flakes or include dried chiles or flakes in the spice bag.
• Use dried cranberries instead of raisins.

Plum Chutney

To accentuate the plum flavor, crack half a dozen of the plum pits to extract the kernels and include these, bruised, with the spices.

PREPARATION **1 HOUR**

COOKING **ABOUT 2 TO 3 HOURS**

Makes 6 cups
2 pounds ripe plums, halved or
   quartered and pits removed and
   set aside
1 pound baking apples, peeled and
   chopped
1½ cups pitted prunes, chopped
1 pound red onions, chopped
2½ cups granulated sugar
1 teaspoon salt
3 cups red wine vinegar
1 tablespoon black peppercorns
10 cloves
5-inch cinnamon stick

1 Put the plums, apples, prunes, and onions into a large nonreactive pan with the sugar, salt, and vinegar.
2 Bruise the peppercorns, cloves, cinnamon, and plum pit kernels (if using) with a mortar and pestle, and tie them loosely in cheesecloth.
3 Put the pan over medium-low heat and stir frequently until the sugar has dissolved completely and some liquid has been drawn from the fruit and vegetables. Add the spice bag and cook the mixture down slowly, stirring more frequently as it thickens.
4 When the chutney is well cooked (about 2 to 3 hours), remove the spice bag and spoon the chutney into sterilized jars and seal.

Green Tomato Chutney (page 124)

Red Tomato and Onion Seed Chutney (page 124)

Plum Chutney

Red Onion Marmalade

Spicy Pear and Pumpkin Chutney

Pear and Pumpkin Chutney

Pickling

A simple sweet or pungent pickle can be created by packing practically any kind of fruit or vegetable into jars and topping it up with cold vinegar. More elaborate concoctions combine aromatic herbs and fragrant spices with sufficient sugar to both soften the tartness and to improve the flavor and texture, which can range from sour to sweet, crisp to tender. When it comes to eating, patience is essential; the longer the pickle can be left to cure the mellower the final result.

The Pickling Larder

A larder packed with pickled vegetables and fruit offers infinite possibilities for simple suppers with cold meats and cheese. Sharp, salty, or sweet-sour, the most appealing ingredients used are either crunchy, such as red cabbage, onions, and gherkins, or sweet, like pears, peaches, and plums. Subtle but satisfying tweaks can be made with a variety of herbs and spices and different flavored vinegars.

Pickled Red Cabbage (page 132)

INGREDIENTS

Vinegar preserves by penetrating food, replacing its natural liquids and inhibiting the growth of microorganisms. It also infuses the food with its own flavor so the pickle will only ever be as good as the quality of vinegar used. **Wine vinegars** are the finest and create delicate, subtle pickles, but the less expensive **cider**, **malt**, and **distilled varieties** also produce delicious, if slightly more robust, results. Check the label to ensure your vinegar has at least 5% acetic acid content for successful preservation.

Sugar is also an important preservative and, depending on the variety, can simply mellow the vinegar or, in the case of **dark brown sugar**, add another dimension to the end result altogether.

Both the vinegar and sugar you choose will affect the final color: distilled or white wine vinegar and white granulated sugar, for example, are ideal for creating clear pickles, and won't alter the natural color of pale produce such as cauliflower or eggs.

Subtle use of **herbs** and **spices** takes pickles to even higher levels. They can be tied in a cheesecloth bag to infuse during preparation, strained before final pickling, or added to the jars for interest. Always use whole spices as ground versions cloud the vinegar.

EQUIPMENT

Happily, pickle making doesn't require specialized equipment. However, all utensils and containers should be **stainless steel**, **glass**, or **enamel**, with a **nylon strainer** for straining because the acid in vinegar reacts with certain metals, turning pickles bitter. **Kilner jars** or **jam jars** with **vinegar-proof lids** make good containers, or traditional **large pickle jars**. Sterilize them in the hottest cycle of your dishwasher or wash in hot, soapy water, then put in the oven at 300°F for 20 minutes. The pickles must remain submerged in the vinegar—if they're bobbing above the liquid a disk of **wax paper** will hold them below the surface.

A BIT OF TECHNIQUE

• There are two methods of pickling: hot and cold. For the former, vinegar is brought to a boil with flavorings and poured over vegetables, enabling it to penetrate more quickly and soften them slightly—particularly good for large, firm vegetables, such as beet. Alternatively, cold vinegar is simply poured over vegetables, such as cauliflower, to keep them crunchy.

• Salt also plays an important role in pickling techniques because it helps to draw out excess moisture and keep vegetables crisp. Dry salting is used when pickling delicate vegetables, such as cucumber. Slices are sprinkled with salt and left for 24 hours. Then they are rinsed, dried, and packed into jars with vinegar. As a rule, allow 3 tablespoons salt for each 14 ounces vegetables.

• A brine (wet salting) is used for firmer vegetables, such as pickling onions, and is left for 24 hours before rinsing. Allow 3 tablespoons salt for every 2½ cups water—it should be buoyant enough to be able to float a fresh egg in it.

Pickled Shallots

Shallots have a slightly more delicate flavor than their robust cousins, pickling onions.

PREPARATION **40 MINUTES PLUS STANDING**
COOKING **10 MINUTES**

Makes 3 pounds
1 pound 9 ounces shallots, peeled and trimmed
5 tablespoons sea salt
2½ cups boiling water
2½ cups distilled vinegar
¾ cup dark brown sugar
1 blade of mace
½ teaspoon each Sichuan and black peppercorns,
 plus extra for the jars
1 star anise, plus extra for the jars
bay leaves, for the jars

1 Put the shallots and salt into a large nonmetallic bowl and add the boiling water. Cover and let stand overnight.
2 Put the remaining ingredients into a pan. Bring to the boil and simmer for 5 minutes.
3 Drain the shallots and add to the pan. Simmer for 5 minutes, until transparent but still crisp. Remove with a slotted spoon.
4 Pack sterilized jars two-thirds full with the shallots. Pour over the hot vinegar, adding a few peppercorns to each jar, a star anise, and a bay leaf. Store in a cool, dark place for 1 month before eating.

Pickled Red Cabbage

Serve this vibrantly colored, crunchy pickle with stews and roast meats, or a good home-cooked slice of cold ham.

PREPARATION **15 MINUTES PLUS SALTING**
COOKING **5 MINUTES**

Makes about 3 pounds
1 red cabbage, cored and roughly shredded
sea salt
3 cups red wine vinegar
2 cups Raspberry Vinegar (see page 142)
3 large bay leaves
6 cloves
12 juniper berries

1 Layer the cabbage in a bowl, sprinkling with salt as you go. Cover and let stand overnight.
2 Rinse the cabbage, pat dry, and pack into sterilized jars.
3 Put the remaining ingredients into a pan and boil for about 3 minutes. Pour the hot vinegar over the cabbage so that it is submerged—just add more vinegar if there isn't enough. Seal and store in a cool, dark place for 1 month before eating.

Fruit Mustard Pickle

An unusual sweet and hot fruit pickle originating from Northern Italy called *mostarda di frutta*, where it is served with boiled meat, but equally delicious with cured meats.

PREPARATION **30 MINUTES PLUS STANDING**
COOKING **30 MINUTES**

Makes about 2 pounds
4 ¼ cups granulated sugar
⅔ cup water
1 small lemon and 2 limes, sliced
1½ cups plums, halved and pitted
1 cup black grapes
1½ cups cubed or balled melon
1½ cups peeled, cored, and chopped pineapple
⅔ cup white wine vinegar
3 tablespoons English mustard powder

1 Put 3 cups of the sugar into a large pan with the water. Melt over gentle heat until the sugar is dissolved.
2 Add the fruit and cook over low heat for 10 to 15 minutes, until it softens slightly. Pour into a bowl.
3 Put the remaining sugar into the pan with the vinegar and simmer for about 15 minutes, until it is thick and syrupy. Let cool.
4 Mix 2 tablespoons of the vinegar mixture with the mustard powder, then stir into the rest of the vinegar. Let thicken for 1 hour.
5 Add the mustard vinegar to the fruit, stir well, and then pack into warm, sterilized jars. Store in a cool, dark place for 2 weeks before eating.

Spiced Oranges

A sweet, spicy pickle that is perfect served with ham. Choose unwaxed oranges if you can find them or scrub thoroughly before cooking to remove the wax coating.

PREPARATION **30 MINUTES PLUS STANDING**
COOKING **1 HOUR 20 MINUTES**

Makes about 3 pounds
10 thin-skinned oranges
2½ cups white wine vinegar
5 cups granulated sugar
1 large cinnamon stick
4 allspice berries
about 12 cloves

1 Cut the oranges into ¼-inch slices. Put in a pan and cover with cold water. Simmer for 30 to 40 minutes, until the peel is tender.
2 Put the remaining ingredients in another pan and heat gently until the sugar is dissolved. Bring to a boil for 2 minutes.
3 Remove the orange slices with a slotted spoon, reserving the poaching liquid, and put into the vinegar mixture. Let simmer for about 30 minutes, until the oranges are translucent. Let stand in the liquid overnight.
4 The next day, simmer the oranges again until they are completely tender. Put into sterilized jars and cover with the syrup. Keep the poaching liquid in the refrigerator and use to top up the orange slices if they absorb some of the vinegar syrup. Store in a cool, dark place for 6 weeks before eating.

Pickled Quail Eggs

A tasty little snack or accompaniment to curries, these pickled quail eggs are incredibly addictive.

PREPARATION **20 MINUTES PLUS COOLING**
COOKING **5 MINUTES**

Makes about 1 pound
1 ¼ cups cider vinegar
¾-inch piece of fresh ginger, sliced
½ tablespoon coriander seeds
2 dried red chiles
½ tablespoon black peppercorns
24 quail eggs

1 Put all the ingredients except the eggs in a pan. Bring to a boil, then let simmer for 5 minutes. Let cool completely.
2 Gently bubble the eggs in simmering water for 2½ minutes, or until hard-boiled. Cool under cold running water. Peel when cool enough to handle and pack into sterilized jars.
3 Strain the vinegar and pour over the eggs to cover completely. Add a few of the spices for decoration if you like. Seal with vinegar-proof lids. Store in a cool, dark place for 6 weeks before eating.

Aromatic Spiced Pears

Particularly good with cold meats or cheese. Use firm pears such as Bartlett for best results.

PREPARATION **20 MINUTES**
COOKING **ABOUT 30 MINUTES**

Makes about 2 pounds
2½ cups granulated sugar
2 cups distilled vinegar
juice and pared zest of 1 lemon
1 teaspoon allspice berries
1 teaspoon whole cloves
2 small cinnamon sticks
2½ pounds hard pears

1 Put all of the ingredients except the pears into a large pan. Heat gently until the sugar is dissolved, then bring to a boil for 5 minutes.
2 Meanwhile, peel and core the pears, slicing into quarters, halves, or keeping whole, depending on their size.
3 Add the pears to the vinegar mixture and gently poach until just tender—this can take from 5 to 20 minutes depending on their ripeness. Remove with a slotted spoon as they become tender and transfer to hot, sterilized jars.
4 Boil and reduce the vinegar by a third, then strain over the pears, adding some of the whole spices for decoration. Cover the top of the pears with waxed paper to keep them submerged and seal with a vinegar-proof lid. Store in a cool, dark place for at least 1 month before eating.

Bottling and Liqueurs

Capturing the essence of produce picked at the height of perfection, luscious bottled fruits and fresh, clean tasting cordials bring welcome cheer to the table. At harvest time, the country kitchen would traditionally be a hive of activity, turning home-grown and foraged food into a stock of delicious pantry treats for long winter days. Sadly, this thrifty practice has fallen out of favor since the advent of freezers, but deserves to be revived. Not only does it have a virtue of economy by preserving goods when at their most abundant, but it also tastes far superior to anything similar purchased out of season.

Bottling

Whether it's harvesting an orchard glut of fruit, infusing the flavor of delicate herbs in oil or vinegar, or capturing the deep savory taste of mushrooms in a ketchup, there is still a place for bottling in the modern country kitchen. Preserving by this method isn't complicated if the simple rules are followed. Most agreeably for the cook, it stocks up the pantry with exciting and versatile food that cheers up the winter table by enabling ingredients to be used out of season with little change to texture and flavor. A touch of planning in the warmer months also enables the dedicated cook to use seasonal produce at its peak to make pleasing Christmas gifts for family and friends.

INGREDIENTS

Bottling is a great way of preserving **delicate fruits** that would be damaged by freezing, keeping their texture and flavor similar to their original state.

Fruit should be firm and just ripe and free from bruises. Remove stalks from small fruits such as **redcurrants** and **gooseberries** and leave whole. Larger fruits such as **apricots** and **peaches** are best halved and pitted; blanch and peel away the skins. **Pears** are low in acid, so 2 teaspoons lemon juice should be added to every 2 cups sugar syrup before processing.

A **sugar syrup** preserves the color and texture of the fruit and once the preserve is opened can be drizzled over ice cream or added to drinks. The strength of syrup depends on personal taste, but a lighter one is more attractive if the preserve is a gift. For a light sugar syrup, dissolve ⅔ cup granulated sugar in 2½ cups water over low heat, then boil for 2 minutes without stirring; for a medium syrup use 1¼ cups sugar to 2½ cups water; for a heavy syrup use a scant 2 cups sugar to 2½ cups water.

Fruit juice or **alcohol**, such as brandy, gin, or vodka, can be substituted for the sugar syrup. **Whole spices** can be added for an extra flavor depth (ground spices will cloud the syrup).

Firm or fibrous fruit such as **apples**, **pears**, and **apricots** benefit from precooking in sugar syrup. Toss in lemon juice first to prevent discoloration.

EQUIPMENT

Jars and **bottles** need to be thicker than normal jam jars to withstand the heating process. **Clip jars** have glass lids fitted with rubber rings and a metal clip to seal; **screw-top (Kilner) jars** are sealed with metal lids and a separate metal screw band. A **deep pan** and **thermometer** are necessary if you plan to process the jars using the water bath method, otherwise a large **baking sheet** or **roasting pan** may be used for the oven method.

A BIT OF TECHNIQUE

• All equipment should be scrupulously clean to prevent contamination. Bacteria that cause spoilage are destroyed at temperatures from 165 to 212°F and can be reached by heating raw or cooked produce in a simple water bath or in the oven.
• Acidity is key: the more acid the food contains, the more easily the organisms are destroyed by heat. Low acid foods must be preserved at higher temperatures with specialized equipment to prevent bacterial spores from causing food poisoning, so this is not recommended for the home cook.
• Sterilize jars by running on the hottest cycle of your dishwasher or wash in hot, soapy water, then put on a foil-lined baking sheet in the oven at 300°F for 20 minutes. Sterilize the lids and rubber rings in boiling water.
• To process: fill sterilized jars and put the lids in place. Screw-band lids should be tightened, then unscrewed by a quarter turn. Fit clip jars with the rubber ring and position the clip over the hinge to hold the lid in place if using the oven method or clamp in place if using the water bath technique.
• To process jars or bottles in the oven, space them apart on a newspaper-lined baking sheet. Put in the oven at 300°F for the specified time. Remove and tighten the screw lids or clips at once.
• To process jars or bottles in a water bath, space apart on a trivet set in a large, deep pan. Pour in enough warm water to cover the jars by 1 inch. Cover the pan with a lid and slowly bring to a simmer for the required length of time. Remove and tighten the lids or clips immediately.

PROCESSING TIMES

Only foods with a high level of acidity can be processed at home safely. If using the water bath process, warm water must be slowly brought to a particular temperature over 25 minutes and held there for a specified length of time (see chart opposite).

TESTING FOR A SEAL

Let stand for 24 hours. The screw-top jars should make a seal as they cool—the lid should look slightly concave. Press the top with a finger and if it pops up, it has not sealed. To test clip jars, undo the clip and try to open the lid with a fingernail; if it remains in place then the seal is airtight. If the seal hasn't worked, store the jar in the refrigerator and eat the contents within two weeks. Immediately before consuming the contents, check the seal is still effective before opening. If a jar lid ruptures or pops up during storage the contents should be discarded.

Opposite: Bottled Rhubarb with Orange and Ginger (page 140)

BOTTLING TIMES

Produce	Oven method (minutes)	Water bath method (minutes and temperature)
Apple slices	30 40	2 @ 165°F
Apricots, halved	40–50	20 @ 180°F
Blackberries	30–40	2 @ 165°F
Blackcurrants	30–40	2 @ 165°F
Blueberries	30–40	2 @ 165°F
Cherries	40–50	10 @ 180°F
Citrus fruit	30–40	10 @ 165°F
Cranberries	30–40	2 @ 165°F
Gooseberries	40–50	2 @ 165°F
Nectarines, halved	50–60	20 @ 180°F
Peaches, halved	50–60	20 @ 180°F
Pears, halved	60	60 @ 190°F
Plums, halved	50–60	20 @ 180°F
Quinces, sliced	40–50	30 @ 190°F
Raspberries	30–40	2 @ 165°F
Redcurrants	30–40	2 @ 165°F
Rhubarb	40–50	2 @ 165°F
Tomatoes, whole	60–80	50 @ 190°F

Bottled Clementines

A ready-made sauce for drizzling over pancakes.

PREPARATION **20 MINUTES PLUS PROCESSING**

Makes 1¾ pints
⅔ cup granulated sugar
2½ cups water
10–12 clementines
3 cloves
1 small stick cinnamon

1 Dissolve the sugar in the water in a saucepan over gentle heat, then boil for 2 minutes without stirring to make a sugar syrup. You may not need all of the syrup but it will keep for several weeks in a container in the refrigerator. Peel the clementines and leave whole. Peel away any white pith.
2 Pack one-third of the fruit into a large sterilized jar and pour in enough hot syrup to cover. Add the cloves and cinnamon. Add another third of the clementines and syrup to cover. Repeat until all the fruit is used, ensuring there is a 1-inch gap at the top. Completely cover the fruit with syrup.
3 Seal the jar and heat process in a water bath for 10 minutes at 165°F or in the oven for 30 to 40 minutes (see page 138).
4 Check the seal before storing in a cool, dark place. Store in the refrigerator once opened and use within 1 month.

Bottled Rhubarb with Orange and Ginger

Drizzle the juices over ice cream or use in cocktails.

PREPARATION **20 MINUTES PLUS PROCESSING**

Makes about 1¼ pints
1¼ cups granulated sugar
2½ cups water
juice of 1 large orange
1 pound rhubarb
¾-inch piece of fresh ginger, peeled and sliced

1 Dissolve the sugar in the water in a saucepan over gentle heat, then boil for 2 minutes without stirring to make a sugar syrup. Stir in the orange juice.
2 Slice the rhubarb into chunks and pack it into sterilized jars along with the sliced ginger.
3 Pour over the hot sugar syrup to cover. Seal the jar and heat process in a water bath for 2 minutes at 165°F or in the oven for 40 to 50 minutes (see page 138).
4 Check the seal before storing in a cool, dark place. Store in the refrigerator once opened and use within 1 month.

Cherries in Brandy

Most soft fruits can be bottled in alcohol and because the spirit acts as a preservative there is no need to heat process the sterilized jars after sealing.

1 Prick each cherry with a needle. You can remove the pits from the fruit, or not, as you like. Pack the cherries into a sterilized, wide-mouth, preserving jar with the spices.

2 Add the sugar to the jar and pour over the brandy. Seal and gently turn the jar to help dissolve the sugar.

3 Store in a cool, dark place for 2 months before eating, turning once a week for the first month to ensure the sugar is dissolved. The longer you leave the fruit to age, the better it will taste. Store in the refrigerator once opened and use within 6 months.

PREPARATION **15 MINUTES**

Makes 2 pounds
2 pounds sweet cherries
6 cloves
1 cinnamon stick
1 blade of mace
1¾ cups granulated sugar
about 3 cups brandy

Basil Oil

A few sprigs of rosemary, thyme, or tarragon could replace the basil.

PREPARATION **10 MINUTES PLUS STANDING**

Makes 2½ cups
a handful basil leaves
2½ cups olive oil

1 Put the ingredients into a large jar or bowl, making sure the herbs are submerged. Cover with a lid or plastic wrap and let stand in a cool, dark place for 1 month, swirling occasionally.
2 Strain the oil into sterilized bottles. Add an herb sprig if you like and seal. Store in a cool, dark place for up to 6 months.

Tarragon Vinegar

This is an essential ingredient for a classic béarnaise sauce.

PREPARATION **10 MINUTES PLUS STANDING**

Makes 2 cups
3 large sprigs fresh tarragon
2 cups white wine vinegar

1 Put the ingredients into a large jar or bowl, making sure the herbs are submerged. Cover with a lid or plastic wrap and let stand in a cool, dark place for 2 weeks, swirling occasionally.
2 Strain into sterilized bottles. Add an herb sprig for decoration and seal. Store in a cool, dark place for up to 1 year.

Raspberry Vinegar

If fresh raspberries are out of season, use defrosted frozen raspberries.

PREPARATION **10 MINUTES PLUS STANDING**

Makes about 3 cups
4 cups fresh raspberries
2½ cups white wine vinegar

1 Lightly mash the raspberries in a nonmetallic bowl; stir in the vinegar. Cover the bowl with plastic wrap and let stand in a cool, dark place for 1 week.
2 Strain the mixture through cheesecloth into a bowl, then decant into sterilized bottles with a funnel. Seal and label. Store in a cool place for up to 1 year.

Flavored oils and vinegars are quick to make and don't need to be heat processed. Use them in dressings, stir-fries, and when marinating meat, fish, and vegetables.

Chile Oil

Be aware that chiles vary in their hotness, but if you want a very fiery oil you can add the seeds too.

PREPARATION **10 MINUTES PLUS STANDING**

Makes 2½ cups
9 fresh or dried whole chiles
2½ cups sunflower oil

1 Halve and seed the fresh chiles or split the dried chiles. Pack them into a large jar or bowl and pour over the oil. Cover with a lid or plastic wrap and let stand in a cool, dark place for 2 weeks.
2 When it has reached the desired level of hotness, strain the oil into sterilized bottles. Add a dried chile for decoration if you like and seal. Store in a cool, dark place for up to 6 months.

Tomato Ketchup

Choose very ripe, red tomatoes for the best flavor.

PREPARATION **30 MINUTES**
COOKING **2½ TO 3¾ HOURS**

Makes 4 cups
6 pounds very ripe tomatoes, chopped
2 onions, chopped
1 green pepper, seeded and chopped
⅔ cup light brown sugar
¾ cup distilled vinegar
½ tablespoon paprika
½ tablespoon dry mustard powder

FOR THE SPICE BAG
1 small cinnamon stick
3 black peppercorns
3 allspice berries
6 cloves
½ teaspoon fennel seeds

1 Put the tomatoes, onions, and green pepper in a saucepan and cook for 30 to 40 minutes over low heat until soft. Blend in a blender or food processor, then push through a strainer into a bowl.
2 Tie the whole spices in a piece of cheesecloth to make a spice bag.
3 Put the pureed tomatoes in a large saucepan and add the remaining ingredients and the spice bag. Simmer, covered, for 2 to 3 hours, until thickened but still pourable.
4 Remove the spice bag and pour the tomato mixture into sterilized bottles, leaving a 1-inch gap at the top. Heat process in a water bath for 30 minutes at 183°F or in the oven for 50 minutes (see page 138).
5 Store in a cool, dark place and in the refrigerator once opened. Use within 2 months.

Mushroom Ketchup

Add a dash to casseroles and pie mixtures for extra depth of flavor.

PREPARATION **30 MINUTES**
COOKING **1½ TO 2 HOURS**

Makes about 3 cups
10 cups mushrooms, finely chopped
1 pack dried wild mushrooms, about 1 ounce
¼ teaspoon ground cloves
½ teaspoon ground mace
½ teaspoon ground allspice
2 anchovy fillets
1¼ cups Madeira
5 tablespoons water

1 Put all of the ingredients into a large saucepan with the water and bring to a boil. Simmer very gently, uncovered, for about 1 hour.
2 Strain the mixture through a cheesecloth-lined strainer into a bowl, squeezing out as much juice as possible.
3 Return the liquid to the saucepan and boil to reduce over medium heat to the consistency you prefer—thicker for a condiment, thinner if to be used as a flavoring for soups and stocks.
4 Pour into sterilized bottles and store in a cool, dark place for 3 months. Refrigerate once opened and use within 6 months. To extend the life of the ketchup for up to 1 year, process with the water bath method to 212°F for 20 minutes or in the oven for 50 minutes (see page 138).

Liqueurs and Cordials

Homemade cordials and liqueurs

are luxurious additions to the country pantry, often made with the most frugal of ingredients. Flowers and berries can be transformed into delightful summer drinks or cordials, while a warming liqueur made from wild plums cheers up the darkest of winter nights and makes a welcome Christmas gift. Homemade liqueurs and cordials need few special tools. Squares of cheesecloth will ensure the cordial is properly strained or a jelly bag can be used for extraclear results. A plastic funnel means not a drop of liquid will be spilled when filling bottles. Glass bottles, fitted with either corks or swing stoppers, make attractive containers, especially if the cordial or liqueur is to be a gift.

Blackcurrant Cordial

Elderflower Cordial

Cranberry and Orange Vodka

A Bit of Technique
Pricking fruit helps to release the juice that flavors the alcohol. Always fill the jar or bottle to the top as any air space causes the liqueur's flavor to dissipate. Keeping the drinks in a cool, dark place prolongs their life and, properly stored, liqueurs will keep for many years and improve with age. Extend the life of cordials for up to a year using the water bath or oven method described on page 138.

Plum Brandy

Wild Plum Brandy

Whisky Liqueur

Elderflower Cordial

Pick elderflowers early in the season for the best flavor

PREPARATION **10 MINUTES PLUS STANDING**

Makes about 4 cups
4½ cups granulated sugar
3½ cups boiling water
5 teaspoons citric acid
juice of 2 lemons
12 to 15 elderflower heads

1 Dissolve the sugar in a large bowl with the water. Stir in the citric acid and lemon juice.
2 Shake the elderflowers to remove any insects, add to the sugar syrup, cover, and let stand for 5 days, stirring daily.
3 Strain through a cheesecloth-lined strainer. Decant into sterilized bottles. It will keep for up to 1 year in the refrigerator. Dilute with water, tonic, or soda water.

Blackcurrant Cordial

Try making this cordial with redcurrants as an alternative.

PREPARATION **10 MINUTES**
COOKING **5 MINUTES**

Makes about 2 cups
4½ cups ripe blackcurrants
⅔ cup water
granulated sugar

1 Put the berries in a pan with the water and cook lightly for 5 minutes, squashing the fruit with a wooden spoon to extract as much juice as possible.
2 Push through a cheesecloth-lined strainer to extract as much juice as possible. Measure and allow 1¾ cups sugar for every 2 cups juice.
3 Dissolve the sugar with the juice over low heat, then pour into sterilized bottles. Store in the refrigerator for up to 2 weeks or process in a water bath for 2 minutes at 165°F or in the oven for 30 to 40 minutes (see page 138).

Plum Brandy

Eat the plums with ice cream once the liqueur is strained.

PREPARATION **20 MINUTES PLUS STANDING**

Makes about 2½ cups
2½ cups brandy
1 pound plums, pierced a few times with a skewer
1½ cups granulated sugar

1 Put the ingredients into a large sealable jar.
2 Store in a cool, dark place, turning gently every day for the first week to help the sugar to dissolve. Let stand for 1 month to age.
3 Strain through a cheesecloth-lined strainer into a bowl. Decant into sterilized bottles, seal, and label.

Whisky Liqueur

An infusion of sugar and spices softens even the harshest whisky into a warming liqueur.

PREPARATION **20 MINUTES PLUS STANDING**

Makes about 2½ cups
2½ cups whisky
thinly pared zest of 1 orange
6 cloves
1 cup dried figs, roughly chopped
½ cup light brown sugar

1 Put the ingredients into a large sealable jar.
2 Store in a cool, dark place, turning gently every day for the first week to help the sugar to dissolve. Let stand for 1 month to age.
3 Strain through a cheesecloth-lined strainer into a bowl. Decant into sterilized bottles, seal, and label.

Cranberry and Orange Vodka

The flavors of Christmas in a glass.

PREPARATION **20 MINUTES PLUS STANDING**

Makes about 4 cups
4 cups vodka
thinly pared zest of 1 orange
1⅓ cups granulated sugar
⅔ cup dried cranberries
1 small cinnamon stick

1 Put the ingredients into a large sealable jar.
2 Store in a cool, dark place, turning gently every day for the first week to help the sugar to dissolve. Let stand for 1 month to age.
3 Strain through a cheesecloth-lined strainer into a bowl. Decant into sterilized bottles, seal, and label.

Wild Plum Brandy

You can replace the brandy with gin if you prefer.

PREPARATION **15 MINUTES**

Makes about 3½ cups
1 pound wild plums
1 cup superfine sugar
3 cups brandy

1 Prick the wild plums with a needle a few times. Put into a large wide-mouth jar.
2 Add the sugar and brandy and stir well. Strain through a cheesecloth-lined strainer into a bowl. Decant into sterilized bottles, seal, and label. Store in a cool, dark place for 3 months, shaking gently once a week.

Wild Plum Brandy, Ginger, and Apple Punch

Serve this refreshing long drink with plenty of ice, mint sprigs, and lemon slices.

PREPARATION **10 MINUTES**

Makes about 10 cups
2 cups Wild Plum Brandy (see previous recipe)
4 cups dry ginger ale
4 cups fresh apple juice
juice of 1 lemon
2 tablespoons superfine sugar

Mix all of the ingredients together and serve at once.

Wild Plum Brandy, Ginger, and Apple Punch

Lemon Barley Water

Make an orange barley water with two oranges instead.

PREPARATION **20 MINUTES PLUS STANDING**
COOKING **5 MINUTES**

Makes 6 cups
⅔ cup pearl barley
¼ cup granulated sugar
pared zest and juice of 4 large unwaxed lemons
4 cups boiling water

1 Rinse the pearl barley in several changes of cold water until it runs clear.
2 Put the pearl barley in a pan and cover with cold water. Bring to a boil, then simmer for 5 minutes. Drain and rinse in cold water.
3 Put the pearl barley in a large bowl with the sugar, lemon zest, and the boiling water. Stir to dissolve the sugar, then cover and let infuse until cooled.
4 Strain the pearl barley through a cheesecloth-lined strainer. Stir in the lemon juice and chill. Store in the refrigerator and use within 3 days.

Ginger Beer

Once the ginger has fermented, drink within a couple of days.

PREPARATION **20 MINUTES PLUS STANDING**

Makes about 2 cups
2-inch piece of fresh ginger
4 teaspoons cream of tartar
2 ¼ cups granulated sugar
zest and juice of 1 lemon
4 quarts boiling water
½ tablespoon dry yeast

1 Roughly slice the ginger and put into a large bowl with the cream of tartar, sugar, and lemon zest. Pour in the boiling water. Stir until the sugar is dissolved. Let stand until hand-hot.
2 Add the lemon juice and yeast. Cover; let stand in a warm place for 24 hours.
3 Skim and strain the liquid through a cheesecloth-lined strainer into sterilized swing-stoppered glass bottles.
4 Leave for 2 to 3 days, checking daily to make sure the ginger beer is not too fizzy—loosen the caps if the liquid looks too fizzy to avoid the bottles exploding. Store in the fridge and use within 3 days.

Curing
and Potting

In times past, preserving food was a matter of survival. When the cottager's pig was slaughtered in winter, the meat was hung high up in the chimney to smoke, or transformed into sausages and cured salamis. Fresh fish was smoked, salted, or potted to extend its life and make it unappealing to bacteria. Translucent slices of smoked salmon, magnificent hams, and the finest bacon all owe their tantalizingly complex flavors to these traditional practices. Now, with refrigerators and freezers to take care of safe storage, we can explore what they have to offer simply for our own pleasure.

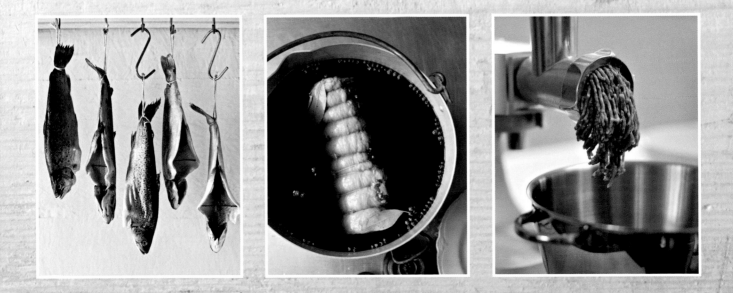

Salting

Country cooks once preserved the family pig in layers of salt to ensure a supply of meat for the winter. Before refrigeration it was the simplest and most widespread technique for preserving food. Although quick and reliable, the meat did need thorough soaking for days on end to make it edible. Consequently, flavor became important, too, and this technique evolved to include sugar, herbs, and spices in the salting mixtures. Modern methods of preservation have rendered salting unnecessary and it is now carried out for flavor alone. But the processes of dry-salting and wet-salting (brining) are simple enough to do in your own kitchen and the results are always pleasing. Dry-salting is the most straightforward and gives quick results: fresh meat or fish is rubbed with a salt mixture and turned every few days. Cheaper cuts of beef respond particularly well to wet-salting, transforming its texture and flavor, while a side of fresh salmon becomes a very special treat for large gatherings or celebrations by dry-salting. A few bags of salt and sugar, a sprinkling of aromatic herbs, and spices and some fresh fish, meat, or vegetables are all you need to create your own very special Gravlax (see pages 156–157), Salt Beef (see pages 160–161), or Dill Pickles (see page 158).

INGREDIENTS

Salt preserves food by drawing out moisture and dissolving in this liquid, preventing growth of potentially harmful microorganisms. Use **sea salt** rather than table salt as the latter contains additives that can cause food to discolor. A **dry salt mix** or **brine solution** (see opposite) can be flavored with **herbs** and **whole spices**. Allspice, mace, pepper, cloves, juniper berries, or coriander add character. Sugar, honey, or molasses add sweetness and depth of flavor. A small amount of **saltpeter** (potassium nitrate or sodium nitrate) can be stirred into the brine or added to the dry salt mix. This was necessary before refrigeration to augment the preserving process—but this merely makes meat look a more appetizing pink rather than a gray color and isn't strictly necessary nowadays. Some research claims that large amounts of saltpeter can be dangerous, so use no more than the minimum effective amount: 1½ teaspoons to every 4 cups salt and 11 pounds meat. If you do use saltpeter, make sure that you rub some sugar over the meat first: even small amounts of saltpeter can harden the flesh and the sugar will keep it soft.

Meat (beef and pork), **poultry** (chicken and turkey), **fish** (salmon, fresh anchovies, herring), and **vegetables** and some **fruits** are suitable for salting. Certain vegetables produce natural lactic bacteria that reacts with salt and ferments (lacto-fermentation); sauerkraut is a good example of this.

EQUIPMENT

Very little equipment is needed, but any that is used should be scalded with boiling water first to sterilize. A **plastic bucket** or large nonmetallic or enamel **container** is good for holding joints of meat and whole fish in brine. To enable the brine to penetrate large pieces of meat more effectively, pierce the meat all over with a **skewer** or **trussing needle**. Smaller food items can be cured in the refrigerator sitting in a **lipped tray** to catch drips, while larger items in brine that can't be chilled should be stored in a cold, airy environment—a north-facing pantry or garage is ideal—but this is best done during the cooler months of the year. The ideal temperature is 36 to 45°F—low enough to discourage bacterial growth but high enough to enable the salt and juices to mingle and flavor the meat. The longer the

food is left to cure, the stronger the final flavor will be: for meat this can be anything from 2 to 4 weeks and with more delicate fish, 2 to 7 days.

A BIT OF TECHNIQUE

There are two basic methods of preserving food with salt: dry-salting and brining.

• **Dry-salting** involves rubbing salt evenly into food to draw out moisture, which produces a brine. It's most suitable for less bulky cuts so that the salt penetrates rapidly, preventing decay: choose thin pieces of food that can absorb salt quickly, such as vegetables, fish fillets like salmon, or small whole fish such as anchovies.

• Larger pieces of food such as beef brisket or ham can be submerged in a **brine solution**. The brine must be strong enough to extract the juices from the food: a 20 percent salt solution is ideal. It is strong enough if a fresh egg floats on the surface—if it doesn't, keep adding a little more salt until this happens. When salting vegetables, the ingredients must be kept submerged for the fermentation to succeed. You may need to top up the liquid from time to time: make up a light brine of 1½ tablespoons salt mixed with 4 cups water for this purpose.

• Any fish or meat thicker than 2 inches is more easily cured by the brining (wet-salting) method.

• Some dishes such as spiced beef are rubbed with salt and spices and left for 2 to 4 weeks to cure. It is then rinsed and cooked before being ready to eat.

• Fish fillets should be pinboned before curing: gently run your hand over the flesh to feel for bones, then remove any you find with a pair of tweezers.

AN ALL-PURPOSE WET CURE (BRINE)

This brine mix is suitable for most large joints of meat or poultry, even turkey. Make sure that you have enough brine to completely submerge the meat by at least 5 inches—see picture right. Keep it in place with a plate weighed down with weights or cans. Some of the water can be replaced with beer or cider if you prefer.

Put 4 quarts water into a large pan with 6 cups coarse salt, 2½ cups light brown sugar, 1½ teaspoons saltpeter (if using), 2 bay leaves, a large sprig of thyme, 10 crushed peppercorns, and 5 crushed allspice berries. Bring to a boil for 5 minutes. Let cool completely before using.

An all-purpose wet cure (brine)

Gravlax

This is perfect served with thin slices of brown bread and butter and a mustard sauce.

PREPARATION **20 MINUTES PLUS SALTING**

Serves 12
3 pounds salmon, filleted in 2 pieces
2 tablespoons granulated sugar
1 tablespoon sea salt
1 tablespoon finely chopped dill
1 tablespoon gin
8 juniper berries, crushed

1 Choose fillets from the thickest part of the salmon if you can and pinbone if necessary. Put one fillet skin-side down on a large board.
2 Mix together the sugar and salt and spread over the salmon flesh. Sprinkle all over with the dill and the gin and juniper berries, making sure it is evenly covered.
3 Place the other fillet on top, skin-side up. Wrap the fillets up tightly with a large piece of foil. Put in a lipped tray or dish and put another tray or plate on top. Weigh it down with weights or large cans. Put in the refrigerator for 2 to 3 days or up to 1 week, turning every 12 hours.
4 To serve, slice very thinly and enjoy with sour cream and mustard sauce and slices of brown bread and butter.

Dill Pickles

Layer with salt beef for a classic sandwich (see page 161).

PREPARATION **15 MINUTES PLUS SETTING**

Makes about 2 pounds
6 pickling cucumbers, sliced
a few sprigs dill
12 black peppercorns
1 teaspoon celery seeds
2 tablespoons coarse sea salt
2½ cups water

1 Layer the cucumber, dill, peppercorns, and celery seeds in a large sterilized preserving jar.
2 Put the salt in a pan with the water and heat until dissolved. Bring to a boil.
3 Pour enough of the salted boiling water over the cucumber to cover completely. Seal and let set in a cool, dark place for 6 weeks before eating. Store in the refrigerator once opened and use within 2 months.

Preserved Lemons

These lemons can be used in tagines, stews, salads, and salsas. Rinse off the brine first and scoop out the flesh, which will be too salty to eat—the softened, edible lemon skin is all you need to impart flavor.

PREPARATION **15 MINUTES PLUS SETTING**

Makes 2 pounds
7 large thin-skinned unwaxed lemons
⅔ cup coarse sea salt

1 Holding a lemon over a bowl to catch the juice, cut almost lengthwise into quarters, leaving the pieces joined at one end. Remove any seeds you can see. Pack about 1 tablespoon salt into the cuts, then close up the lemon. Put into a sterilized, wide-mouth preserving jar. Repeat with 5 more lemons, packing them tightly into the jar.
2 Juice the remaining lemon and pour into the jar. Sprinkle with any leftover salt and top up with boiling water, making sure the lemons are covered. Seal and store in a cool, dark place for 1 month before using. Store in the refrigerator once opened for up to 1 year.

Baked Chicken with Preserved Lemons

Add a few preserved lemons to a simple one-pan chicken roast dinner for extra depth of flavor.

PREPARATION **20 MINUTES**
COOKING **50 MINUTES**

Serves 4

1 tablespoon olive oil
8 chicken portions, such as thighs and drumsticks
1 preserved lemon (see previous recipe), cut into quarters
1 whole garlic bulb, halved
a small bunch of lemon thyme
salt and freshly ground black pepper

1 Preheat the oven to 400°F. Heat the oil in a large ovenproof roasting pan. Brown the chicken pieces all over.

2 Squeeze the preserved lemons over the browned chicken pieces. Tuck the lemon shells, garlic, and thyme among the chicken pieces in the roasting pan. Season with salt and freshly ground black pepper.

3 Cook in the oven for 40 to 45 minutes, until the chicken pieces are golden and cooked through.

Salt Beef

Delicious served sliced in rye bread with dill pickles (see page 158) and plenty of mustard. Store in the refrigerator for up to 2 weeks.

1 Put all of the ingredients except the meat in a large preserving kettle. Add the cold water and stir to dissolve the sugar and salt. Bring to a boil, then let cool completely.

2 Pierce the beef all over with a skewer and put it into a large container or plastic bucket. Pour over the brine. Weigh it down with a plate topped with cans or weights—the meat should remain submerged. Transfer the container to a cold place for 10 days, checking daily to make sure the meat is still at least ¾ inch under the surface of the brine.

3 Discard the brine, rinse the beef under cold running water, and put it in a large pan. Cover with cold water, bring to a boil, then let simmer for 1 hour.

4 Drain, cover with fresh water, and simmer again for 1 hour. Repeat once more until the beef is extremely tender. Serve hot or let cool in the liquid before slicing if serving cold.

PREPARATION **20 MINUTES PLUS SALTING**
COOKING **3 HOURS**

Serves 8 to 10
3 cups coarse sea salt
2 cups dark brown sugar
1 tablespoon juniper berries, lightly
   crushed
2 teaspoons allspice berries
2 fresh bay leaves
4 quarts cold water
4 pounds beef brisket

Cold Smoking

Cold smoking can transform an otherwise bland food to a delicious treat. Unlike hot smoking, which cooks as well as flavors food, cold smoke works its taste-transforming magic at temperatures too low to cook even the fragile flesh of fish.

In times past, preserving food without refrigeration was a matter of survival, so certainty was more important than subtlety. When the cottager's pig was slaughtered in winter, the hams, bacon sides, and much else were immediately salted down and later dried or hung high up in the chimney to smoke. The salt drew moisture from the meat, dehydrating it and making it unappealing to bacteria. Smoking dried it more and added the inimitable aromas of the wood fire. Well made, bacon and hams remained wholesome for months on end and were often very salty indeed and dry, which is why so many old recipes begin with instructions for a long soak in cold water.

Try soaking a modern mass-produced ham and you'll be lucky if it tastes of anything much by the time it reaches the plate. Industrial practices designed to speed the curing and smoking of factory-farmed meat and fish—such as injecting brine into bacon, which results in the notoriously unpopular white goo in the skillet—have fueled the success of artisan producers who rely on more traditional methods and livestock.

Smoking is usually described as an art. At the domestic level it is more folk art than science and its recipes offer what seem at first to be puzzlingly differing formulas for making, say, bacon or smoked trout. Ingenious people in many places and times and climates, people with different needs and tastes and raw materials, have developed innumerable ways to cure and smoke their food. It is reassuring to discover that so many different ways of doing things work so well.

INGREDIENTS

Read around the subject of curing and you will find passionate opinions and not a lot of science on the merits of **sea** versus **rock salt**. Organic sea salt is as good as salt gets for flavor and I am lucky to have found a local shop that helpfully gets in 50 pound bags to order. Whether sea salt or rock salt, the main thing is that it should be as pure as possible. Cooking salt has some additives but is a better bet than table salt, which usually has more.

Sugar's role in curing is to offset the hardening effect of the salt as well as to add flavor. The darker the sugar, the stronger its effect on the flavor and color of the meat. There are sweet cures where the proportion of sugar to salt goes as high as fifty–fifty—much too sweet for my taste, but maybe just what you have been looking for.

A number of smokers use **briquettes** supplied by their manufacturer. **Sawdust** and **woodchips** can be bought from suppliers of smokers, and once you know what works well, you can look around for a supply of cheap or free wood waste from local sources. **Oak** and **fruitwoods** are prime smoking materials. **Pine** and other **conifers** should be avoided as the wood gives too strong a taint to the smoke.

EQUIPMENT

There is a lot of inexpensive fun to be had creating a **cold smoker** out of a discarded refrigerator or filing cabinet and joining it to a source of smoke by a length of tumble dryer venting hose. And there are tried and tested designs for **wooden or brick-built smokehouses** joined by a subterranean trench or trunking to a fire pit, or made tall enough to cool the smoke as it rises. The challenge they all depend upon is how to keep the smoke-producing woodchips or sawdust smoldering for more than two or three hours at a stretch. So, if you are more interested in food production than in a construction project, buy a smoker. An Internet search should bring up a fairly wide choice. As much by luck as good judgment, I chose the **West Country Cold Smoker**. It has a simple yet sophisticated smoke box that burns reliably for eight hours and, in favorable conditions, for as long as 14 hours on one fill of sawdust. It is big enough to smoke a ham, or four pork bellies, or eight sides of salmon, or a dozen trout. There are also **stacking racks** for smoking small stuff, such as eggs or nuts, and anything that is better smoked lying down than hanging up.

A BIT OF TECHNIQUE

• When cold smoking, the temperature should be kept around 79°F and below 84°F—any higher and you risk the fish disintegrating.

• Brining or dry-salting prior to smoking will firm flesh and improve flavor. It also removes moisture, thereby discouraging bacteria. Fish only needs a short brining period from 30 minutes to 2 to 3 hours depending on the size and how salty you'd like it to taste ultimately.

• To prepare fish for a cold smoker, split from head to tail along the spine. Remove the head and scrape away the gut. Rinse thoroughly, then brine. Let drip-dry for a couple of hours before smoking.

• Make sure that as much surface area of the flesh as possible is exposed to the smoke—the simplest way is to fix the fish tied back to back on nails studded on wooden poles. Allow sufficient space between them to let smoke circulate freely. If you buy a smoker kit, it will contain hanging racks for the fish (see right). Smaller fish, such as sardines, are best smoked on a mesh tray.

• Smoke small fish for 3 to 6 hours and larger, fattier fish for 6 to 10 hours. However, experimentation is the key to smoking. Make copious notes of what you do at each stage so that you can repeat or adjust the process every time to your liking.

• Once smoking is complete, leave the fish in a cool place before chilling. Smoked foods will keep in the refrigerator for at least a week and can also be frozen.

A hanging rack of smoking trout (page 168)

Dry-Cured, Smoked Organic Bacon

Dry-cured, smoked organic bacon is hard to find in one piece and is not difficult to make. It is invaluable as a basis for substantial soups, casseroles, and bean dishes, and makes crisp breakfast strips.

When bacon was made without refrigeration, copious quantities of salt were used to cure it and often saltpeter was added as an additional precautionary preservative, which had the side effect of making the bacon prettily pink. Although it is a permitted preservative, saltpeter (E252, potassium nitrate) has found to be a carcinogen, and its use is now tightly controlled. But there is a modern alternative. Ready-made mixtures of curing salts containing small quantities of sodium nitrite and sodium nitrate also produce rosy pink bacon and ham. They are used in smaller quantities than the recipe that follows, and the curing stage is generally done in vacuum packs under refrigeration. All this is eminently achievable on a domestic scale but does require a vacuum-packing machine.

How salty do you like your bacon? Do you prefer it lightly smoked or pretty pervasive? These are questions of individual taste, and this is where practice pays off. Keep a notebook and learn from your trials and triumphs.

CURING **4 TO 7 DAYS** DRYING **24 TO 48 HOURS**
SMOKING **24 TO 48 HOURS**

Makes about 11 pounds
16 pounds thin end belly of pork, boned and not scored (about 3 or 4 pieces)
4 pounds coarse sea salt
2½ cups raw brown sugar
1 cup juniper berries, crushed (optional)

1 The salted meat will produce copious amounts of liquid and is better raised above it than left sitting in it. Find a plastic box that will hold the pork bellies in a stack and make a few holes around the edge of the base. Set this box in a larger plastic box, raising it a short way off the bottom. Ideally the larger box will have a lid. Note the weight of the pork pieces, together or separately. When they are cured and smoked they may have lost up to 30 percent of their weight.

2 Mix the salt, sugar, and juniper berries thoroughly together. Strew a layer of the salt mixture over the base of the smaller box. Rub a handful of the salt mixture into both sides of the first piece of pork and lay it, flesh side down, in the box. Add the remaining pieces of pork, rubbing the salting mixture into each one before adding it to the stack, and ending with a layer of salt. There will be salt left over.

3 Cover the meat and put the box somewhere cool and dark—a cold larder, garage, or the bottom of the refrigerator. After 2 days, drain off the liquid in the lower box and repack the meat with a little more of the curing mix, rearranging the pieces so that the top one goes to the bottom of the stack and so on.

4 Drain and repack the meat daily for another 2 days, making 5 days' curing in all, by which time the salt should have penetrated to the center of the meat. If the bellies are a bit skinny, reduce this by 1 day, and if they are very thick and fat, or the weather is particularly cold, add 1 to 2 days.

5 Rinse off the salt cure and hang up the bellies to dry in a cool, airy spot for 24 to 48 hours. You now have green bacon. When the surface is dry and a little tacky, it is ready to smoke.

6 Fire up the smoker and hang the bacon pieces in the smoke, making sure that they are not touching each other or the sides. In an ideal world, the temperature in the smoke chamber will be in the 70 to 90°F range. Smoke the bacon for 24 to 48 hours. In cold or very damp weather the smoke penetrates more slowly.

7 You now have smoked bacon. If you can bear the suspense, wait another 24 hours before sampling your efforts. Stored in cool, dry conditions, it will keep for a couple of months or more, longer in the freezer.

Smoked Trout

Farmed trout are sold gutted and gilled, and most of the fish will have lost the plate of bone behind the gills from which they can be suspended, tail down, in the smoker. Trout fishermen, however, have the option of opening the fish down one side of the spine to clean it kipper-fashion, which makes for more even curing and smoking. This is the ideal treatment for fish weighing up to 1 pound each. Larger trout are better smoked in fillets, like sides of smoked salmon.

CURING **ABOUT 5 HOURS PLUS MAKING AND CHILLING THE BRINE**
SMOKING **12 TO 24 HOURS**

Makes 12
12 very fresh trout, gutted weight 10 to 14½ ounces each

FOR THE BRINE
9 cups coarse sea salt
5 quarts water

FOR DRY-SALTING
4 pounds coarse sea salt

1 The brine needs to be well chilled before the fish are added to it, so start the day before. Put the salt and water in a nonreactive container and bring slowly to a boil, stirring to dissolve the salt. Skim, cool, and then chill.
2 Wash and dry the fish and put them in the chilled brine for 3 hours for the smaller fish, 4 for larger ones. Wash them under a cold tap and dry with paper towels.
3 Strew a layer of salt over the base of a clean container large enough to hold the fish in 1 or 2 layers, and pack in the fish, salting them liberally inside and out. Cover them with salt. Let stand in a cool place for just 40 minutes in the case of the smaller fish, 1 hour for larger ones.
4 Wash and dry the fish again. To hang them up, use a trussing needle to thread a loop of string through the flesh near the tail, and tie the string tightly around the tail, making a loop from which to suspend the fish. Pin open the rib cage with toothpicks.
5 Fire up the smoker and hang the fish in it, making sure that they don't touch each other or the sides. Smoke them for 12 to 24 hours, ideally in the temperature range 70 to 79°F— the smoke takes longer to penetrate in cold, damp weather.
6 Fish smoked like this will keep well in the refrigerator for 1 week or more.

Tip
Savor cold-smoked trout like smoked salmon, without further cooking, served with lemon or horseradish cream. But once cold smoked, the freshwater trout resembles sea fish, and is even better cooked either by poaching in milk and served with a poached egg, or simply wrapped loosely in foil and baked for 15 to 25 minutes in an oven preheated to 350°F.

Smoked Trout Fishcakes with Tartare Sauce

These fishcakes are also very good when made with hot-smoked salmon.

1 Cook the potatoes in salted boiling water for 15 to 20 minutes, until tender. Drain and let steam in the colander for 2 minutes to dry out. Mash the potatoes with the butter and mustard. Let stand until cool enough to handle.

2 Carefully stir in the trout and herbs. Divide the mixture into 8 balls, then flatten each ball into a circle about ¾ inch deep.

3 Put the seasoned flour, egg, and breadcrumbs into separate bowls. Dust the fishcakes with flour, dip into the egg, then coat with the breadcrumbs. Let chill for 30 minutes.

4 Meanwhile, make the tartare sauce. Mix together all of the ingredients and season with salt and pepper to taste.

5 Put the oil in a large skillet to the depth of about ¾ inch and set over medium-low heat. Fry the fishcakes for 5 to 6 minutes a side until golden and heated through. Serve with the tartare sauce and lemon wedges.

PREPARATION **35 MINUTES PLUS CHILLING**
COOKING **ABOUT 30 MINUTES**

Serves 4

2 pounds starchy potatoes, such as russet
4 tablespoons (½ stick) butter
1 teaspoon grainy mustard
12 ounces smoked trout, flaked
1 tablespoon each chopped chives and parsley
seasoned flour
2 medium eggs, beaten
1–1½ cups fresh breadcrumbs
sunflower or vegetable oil, for frying
lemon wedges, to serve

FOR THE TARTARE SAUCE
⅔ cup fresh mayonnaise
1 tablespoon capers, rinsed and chopped
6 cornichons, rinsed and chopped
1 shallot, finely chopped
1 tablespoon fresh chopped parsley
a squeeze of lemon juice
salt and freshly ground black pepper

Making Sausages

It is easy to make sausages that taste very good indeed, but a little harder to get the texture right, although that, too, is a matter of personal preference. I want fresh sausages to be succulent and juicy, meaty without being too chewy and certainly not tough. Dried, salami-style sausages, which are not cooked but cured and have big, complex flavors, should be chewy without being leathery, and firm enough to cut into wafer-thin slices. Both fresh and dried sausages start with good pork, at least outdoor-reared and preferably organic. Though breed and diet combine to produce unique flavors, the practical choice is to use the best that's available locally, and not too lean. The beauty of homemade sausages is that they contain only good meat, which includes the fat, and no bits you'd rather not eat if you could identify them. Without sufficient fat, sausages are dry and dull, so fat phobics should read no further and turn their talents to making yogurt or bread. Cooks' perks are the bits that get stuck around the auger of the meat grinder or sausage stuffer. Formed into small, quickly fried patties, they preview the feast to come. And if your taste buds are alert, they also demonstrate the improvement a day's hanging can make to the flavor of a string of homemade sausages.

INGREDIENTS

It is not a bad idea to order the meat in advance, particularly if you need hard pork back fat to dice for dried sausages. The quantities of salt, herbs, and spices used in sausages are small, so why not use the best—**fine sea salt**, freshly ground **peppercorns**, and **fresh herbs**? **Sausage skins** can be natural casings—cleaned intestines preserved in salt—or manufactured casings made from animal collagen. The best casings are natural as they are stronger and more porous than synthetic versions. Hog casings are the size for traditional sausages, and sheep casings for slimmer chipolatas. Larger sizes are needed for dried sausages that will shrink by about a third as they cure. Beef middles are a larger casing, good for homemade salamis when curing temperatures can't be accurately controlled and when the meat needs to be tightly packed to stop harmful bacteria from developing in air pockets. The point being that the bigger and, particularly, thicker the sausage, the longer it takes to cure and the greater the risk of failure—going off or growing the wrong molds before ready.

Specialized ingredients are used in dried sausages to inhibit the growth of harmful organisms during the slow curing process. As the sausages dry, they will develop a white mold on the surface—this is harmless and a good sign that they are aging properly. **Curing salts**, which replace the saltpeter in old recipes, and **salami starter** are available with instructions by mail order. **Acidophilus powder** can be liberated from capsules sold by pharmacies. For casings, ingredients, and equipment, see page 192.

EQUIPMENT

Sausage making demands high standards of kitchen hygiene and keeping every item of equipment spotlessly clean. Although it is possible to make sausages with just a **knife** to chop the meat and a **funnel** to fill the sausage skins, that really is doing things the hard way, and I'd say a **meat grinder** and **sausage stuffer** are essential. I use the grinding attachment of my trusty electric food mixer, which has three sharp metal cutting discs with fine, medium, and coarse holes, and plastic sausage-stuffing nozzles in two sizes. Alternatives include a **hand-cranked grinder** plus a **hand-cranked sausage stuffer**, or powered versions of both, which are larger and designed for farm shop or artisan producer use. You'll also need an accurate **scale** and **measuring cups**, **sharp knives**, scrubbable **boards**,

adequate refrigerator space, and plenty of hot water. In this case, a clean apron to protect the food not your clothing. To make cured sausages, you will need a **cool, dark, well-ventilated area** so that they can be left to hang and dry for several weeks. Try to maintain a constant temperature between 50°F and 59°F to prevent uneven drying. To prevent the sausages from bulging as they are drying, turn them upside down a few times during the first few weeks.

STUFFING SAUSAGES

- The salted sausage casings need to be soaked in warm water for about 30 minutes before attaching one end to a tap and running cold water through its length to rinse thoroughly.
- Allow a good 6½ feet of hog casing per 2 pounds of sausage meat.
- Slide the wet casing onto the sausage-stuffing nozzle of a stand mixer or sausage stuffer and place a large clean tray underneath to collect the sausages.
- For the next stage, two pairs of hands are useful. Fill the machine with the prepared sausage meat and start the motor or crank manually.
- As soon as the sausage mixture begins to come through, tie a knot in the casing and, gently holding it back against the nozzle, let the casing fill plumply.
- To make the links, twist 6–8 inch lengths in alternate directions as they fill.
- Traditionally, sausages and salamis are made in cold winter weather when flies are scarce. To protect fresh sausages I fashioned a simple hanging larder rather like a fisherman's net from a pair of hula hoops and a length of curtain net. Making salami is still best saved for the cooler months.

A BIT OF TECHNIQUE

- Careful cooking ensures succulent, well-flavored sausages. Overcooking dries and toughens them. Whether baked, fried or broiled, aim to cook sausages to an internal temperature of 158°F.
- Lightly cooking onions or garlic in a little butter before adding (chilled) to a sausage mix makes for a richer, more subtle flavor than adding them raw.

Top left: grinding shoulder of pork.
Top right: adding water to the sausage.
Bottom left: soaking the sausage casings before use.
Bottom right: filling the casings until plump.

Sausages with Beans and Rosemary

This dish works well with most flavors of fresh sausages; the beans can be varied to suit your taste.

PREPARATION **20 MINUTES**
COOKING **45 MINUTES**

Serves 4
2 tablespoons sunflower oil
8 fresh sausages (see previous recipe)
1 onion, chopped
1 celery stick, chopped
1 garlic clove, crushed
1 teaspoon tomato paste
1 teaspoon fennel seeds
1 (15-ounce) can chopped tomatoes
1 bay leaf
a pinch of sugar
salt and freshly ground black pepper
1 (10-ounce) can cannellini beans, drained and rinsed
1 (10-ounce) can borlotti beans, drained and rinsed
chopped fresh rosemary leaves, to garnish

1 Heat half the oil in a large sauté pan over medium heat and brown the sausages. Set aside.
2 Add the remaining oil and gently sauté the onion and celery for 10 minutes, or until softened. Add the garlic, tomato paste, and fennel seeds and cook for 1 minute.
3 Pour in the tomatoes, an empty tomato can full of water, and the bay leaf. Add the sugar and season well with salt and pepper. Bring to a boil, then reduce to a simmer. Add the sausages and cook for 25 minutes.
4 Add the beans and continue cooking for 5 minutes, or until heated through. Sprinkle with the rosemary and serve.

Best Classic Sausages

Make the sausages with fatty shoulder of pork, or with half lean pork shoulder and half fatty belly of pork.

PREPARATION **1½ HOURS PLUS CHILLING AND DRYING**

Makes 2½ pounds sausages
2 pounds fatty shoulder of pork without skin or bones
1–1½ teaspoons sea salt
1 generous teaspoon freshly ground black or white pepper
1 teaspoon freshly grated nutmeg
6 tablespoons chilled water
2 cups fresh white breadcrumbs

1 Cut the meat into large dice or strips that will feed easily through the grinder. Combine with the salt, pepper, and nutmeg and mix. Cover and let chill for at least 12 hours.
2 Keeping everything as cold as possible, grind the mixture through the fine or medium holes of a meat grinder.
3 Mix for 1 minute, stirring briskly with a wooden spoon, or use a stand mixer with its mixing paddle on low speed.
4 Increasing the speed to medium, add the water and mix for 1 minute, or until the liquid is incorporated. Sprinkle over the breadcrumbs and mix for another minute until they are well blended in and the mixture is firm and rather sticky.
5 Sauté a teaspoonful of the sausage meat (keeping the bulk chilled) to test for seasoning and adjust it if needed. Be sure to mix in any additional seasoning very thoroughly.
6 Stuff into prepared hog casings, twisting every 6–8 inches. Cook and eat the sausages freshly made. Alternatively, they will keep, hung in a cool, airy place, for between 12 hours and 2 days, depending on the temperature.

Tip
For a quick one-pan meal, put the Classic Sausages in a roasting pan with 1 tablespoon sunflower oil. Add a couple of red onions, cut into wedges, and a few bay leaves. Season with salt and pepper. Bake in the oven at 400°F for 25 to 30 minutes, turning occasionally, until golden and cooked through.

French Country Sausages

This is an all-meat sausage, robustly flavored with wine and garlic, and just the job for a cassoulet.

PREPARATION 1½ HOURS PLUS CHILLING AND DRYING

Makes 2½ pounds sausages
2 pounds fatty shoulder of pork without skin or bones
1–1½ teaspoons sea salt
1 generous teaspoon coarsely ground black pepper
1 tablespoon very finely chopped garlic
6–7 tablespoons robust red wine, chilled

1 Cut the meat into large dice or strips that will feed easily through the meat grinder. Combine the meat with the salt, pepper, and garlic and mix thoroughly. Cover and let chill for at least half a day and up to 24 hours.

2 Keeping everything as cold as possible, grind the mixture through the fine or medium holes of a meat grinder into a bowl.

3 Mix for 1 minute, stirring vigorously with a wooden spoon, or using a stand mixer fitted with its basic mixing paddle on low speed.

4 Increasing the mixer speed to medium, add the wine and mix for another minute, until the liquid is incorporated and the mixture is sticky.

5 Sauté a teaspoonful of the mixture (keeping the bulk chilled) to test the seasoning and adjust it if needed—making sure to mix in any additional seasoning very thoroughly.

6 Stuff into prepared hog casings, twisting every 6–8 inches. Hang the sausages in a cool, airy place for between 12 hours and 2 days, depending on the temperature.

Basic Salami

Salami is an inspired way of preserving meat without refrigeration.

PREPARATION **1½ HOURS PLUS CHILLING**
DRYING **4 OR MORE WEEKS**

Makes 1 pound 7 ounces salami
1 pound 10 ounces lean organic pork
  shoulder
¾ cup finely diced pork back fat
1 teaspoon freshly ground black pepper
1 teaspoon fennel seeds, coarsely
  crushed
2 teaspoons finely ground sea salt
1 garlic clove, crushed to a paste
1 teaspoon acidophilus powder
  or salami starter (see page 172)
6–7 tablespoons robust red wine

1 Grind the pork coarsely into a chilled bowl and add the fat. Sprinkle with the pepper and fennel seeds. Mix the salt, garlic, and acidophilus powder or salami starter with the wine in a small container and stir until the salt has dissolved. Add the liquid to the meat and mix very thoroughly to distribute it evenly. Chill for several hours or overnight, then mix again before filling the casings.
2 Soak and rinse the casings, ideally beef middles, and slide a length onto the sausage-stuffing nozzle. Knot the end of the casing, then above this, tie on a 10-inch piece of string. Fill a 12-inch length and, leaving enough unfilled casing to tie another knot, cut it off. Squeeze the wet filling down firmly before knotting the end and securing this by tying another length of string to it.
3 With a sterile pin, prick the filled skins to puncture any air pockets. Note the weight of each sausage.
4 Hang the salamis in a cool place to dry (ideally 59°F), avoiding extremes of humidity or lack of it, for 4 or more weeks. They are ready when they feel firm right to the center and have lost about 30 percent of their weight.

Tip
Once the salami is ready to eat, it can be wrapped in wax paper and refrigerated. Rolling in fine wood ash from a log fire is a traditional added preservative. Vacuum packing also prolongs the life of cured sausages.

Saucisson Sec

A coarsely cut and simply seasoned French country sausage that allows the quality of good pork to shine.

PREPARATION **1 HOUR PLUS CHILLING**
DRYING **4 OR MORE WEEKS**

*Makes about 1 pound 7 ounces
saucisson sec*
2 pounds organic boneless shoulder of
  pork, chilled
3½ ounces pork back fat, chilled
2 teaspoons finely ground sea salt
1½ teaspoons coarsely ground black
  pepper
2 teaspoons sugar
½ teaspoon curing salts (organic
  dry-cure for bacon)
1 garlic clove, crushed to a paste

1 Grind the pork and fat coarsely into a chilled bowl. Add the remaining ingredients and mix very thoroughly. Chill for several hours or overnight, then mix very thoroughly again before filling the casings.
2 Fill, finish, and dry as for salami.

Terrines and Pâtés

A pork pie is a pâté because it is baked in a pastry crust, and brawn is a terrine because it is set in a dish. At least that is the theory. But both words have for so long been interchangeable that the distinction is obsolete and French cooks resort to the belt and braces *pâté en croûte* when a pastry shell is called for. If you are now pondering the persistence of the French terms pâté and terrine in plain-speaking kitchens, you may agree that cold meat loaf just doesn't cut it. Why make your own when the deli counter has so many to choose from? For all the usual good reasons—superb flavors, economy, and good ingredients with no dodgy bits or dubious additives. Then there's the panache of putting a big dish of pâté on the table with crusty bread, a bowl of salad, and a bottle of wine.

Terrine of Duck (pages 182–183)

INGREDIENTS

Pâtés and terrines are traditionally made with cheaper cuts of meat, such as **belly of pork** and **offal,** particularly **liver.** Fat is a virtue in pâté mixtures, especially when liver and lean meats are used, too. It is traditional to line terrines with fat—often thin slices of **bacon** or **pancetta,** since it has become so difficult to procure pork caul (the fatty membrane from a pig's stomach) or back fat. However, it is worth talking to your butcher, who should be able to order some for you. **Pork fat** is preferable as it has a fairly neutral taste that will mingle well with other flavors and retains a smooth, firm texture and white color during cooking. An easy alternative is to line the dish with plastic wrap.

Buy only the freshest specimens for a **fish terrine**. The raw flesh tends to be sieved for a fine texture, then combined with **eggs, cream,** and **herbs** before being cooked in a bain-marie. The result is a delicate mousse just firm enough to slice. **Salmon** is the most popular type of fish-based terrine.

Vegetable terrines are a colorful, fresh alternative but are best served on the day they're made. They're usually created with three different precooked chopped or pureed vegetables, combined with eggs and herbs. Again, they are gently cooked in a bain-marie where the egg sets and binds the layers. Blanched whole vegetables such as asparagus, green beans, and broccoli florets can also be layered in among the purees.

Small amounts of **wine** and **spirits,** such as **brandy,** add great flavor and, of course, the alcohol cooks off completely. **Spices,** as always, are most fragrant when freshly ground.

EQUIPMENT

A **meat grinder** is the tool of choice for making most types of pâté. For smooth, creamy mousselines or parfaits—mixtures that would once have been worked through a sieve—a **food processor** is invaluable. However, be careful not to overprocess—the end result should be a puree rather than a paste. It does take time and extra elbow grease but if I'm making a fish terrine I will always **sieve** the mixture rather than use a food processor—it's worth it for the light and airy texture.

A **terrine** takes its name from the earthenware dish it was traditionally cooked in. They are usually a narrow rectangular shape, with deep sides tapering slightly toward the base, and holding between 2 pounds and 3 pounds. These are ideal for producing pretty slices of layered ingredients. **Loaf pans** without seams can be substituted, as can small casseroles.

A probe **thermometer** with a digital readout takes the guesswork out of cooking temperatures—so there is no longer any need to play safe and risk overcooking the pâté, which results in too much of the fat melting out and leaving the body of the mixture dry and crumbly. Alternatively, test for doneness by inserting a **skewer** into the center and holding it there for 10 seconds; if the terrine is cooked through the skewer will be hot. A **wooden board** and **heavy scale weights** are used for pressing the terrine after it is cooked—heavy cans make a good substitute.

A BIT OF TECHNIQUE

• Chilling ingredients, grinder, and mixer tools, and keeping everything cold until it goes into the oven, helps to improve the texture of the finished pâté.
• Pick over the meat well before grinding or layering as whole strips: gristle, membrane, or fibrous strands won't grind properly or be pleasant to chew in the finished dish.
• Terrines tend to be cooked in a water bath (bain-marie), which is just a large roasting pan deep enough to contain the terrine. Sufficient boiling water is poured around the terrine to come halfway up the sides, then the dish is put into the oven to cook. Cooking the terrine in this way means that the heat is distributed at an even, gentle rate throughout the dish. Top up with extra boiling water if necessary.
• Seasoning needs to be assertive in dishes eaten cold, so always cook a spoonful of the mixture to check. It is best to poach the test piece wrapped up in plastic wrap, then allow it to cool before tasting. Return the bulk of the mixture back to the refrigerator to keep cold.
• Terrines benefit from resting and chilling in the refrigerator after cooking for a couple of days to allow the flavors to mingle.

Clarifying Butter

Butter has a lower burning point than other fats, but clarifying it first enables you to use it to sauté food at higher temperatures. To make clarified butter, melt a block of butter in a small pan over low heat until liquid. It will separate into three layers: white foam, a thick yellow middle layer, and a milky white sediment at the bottom. Skim off the white foam and discard. Carefully pour off the yellow clarified butter into a bowl. Discard the sediment.

Terrine of Duck

Leave plenty of time for making this terrine before serving: once it's cooked, it needs a couple of days in the refrigerator to allow the flavors to mingle.

PREPARATION 1½ HOURS PLUS CHILLING
COOKING **ABOUT 2 HOURS**

Makes about 2½ pounds

1 duck, about 4 pounds, ideally with
  giblets
2 tablespoons brandy or Calvados
1 pound belly of pork
8 ounces duck or chicken livers, cleaned
⅓ cup finely chopped shallot
1 garlic clove, finely chopped
2 teaspoons each sea salt and freshly
  ground black pepper
6 tablespoons white port or dry
  white wine
1 bay leaf
a few juniper berries, to decorate

FOR THE STOCK

the duck carcass, skin and giblets, and
  skin from the pork belly (if available)
1 small leek, chopped
1 carrot, chopped
2 celery sticks, chopped
2 fresh thyme sprigs
a handful of parsley
1 bay leaf
⅔ cup dry white wine
½ teaspoon salt
½ teaspoon black peppercorns

TO FINISH

½ cup well-flavored duck stock
  (see above)
1 teaspoon powdered gelatin
  (if needed, see method)

1 Cut the legs and wings from the duck, and remove the breast meat, then skin it. Slice the breast meat lengthwise into strips about ½ inch wide. Put them in a dish with the brandy or Calvados, cover, and let chill for 1 to 2 hours or, ideally, overnight.

2 Take the leg and wing meat off the bones and keep it cold.

3 To make the stock, put the carcass, skin, giblets (except the heart and liver), and pork skin in a stockpot and cover with cold water. Bring slowly to a boil, skim, add the vegetables, herbs, wine, and the salt and peppercorns, and let simmer for 2 hours. Strain, discard the solids, skim off the fat, return to the pan, and reduce slowly over medium heat to about 1½ cups. Cool and then chill it. If the stock included the pork skin, it should set to firm jelly by itself. If not, add the gelatin when melting the stock to seal the terrine (see step 10).

4 Meanwhile, preheat the oven to 300°F.

5 Using the fine blade of the meat grinder, grind the meat from the duck legs and wings with the pork, livers, and duck heart and liver if you have them. Add the shallot, garlic, salt, pepper, and port or wine. Stir vigorously, by hand or machine, until the mixture holds together in a sticky mass.

6 Cook (preferably poach, see page 180) a spoonful of the mixture to test for seasoning. If more is needed, be sure to mix it in very thoroughly.

7 Line a 2½-pound dish with plastic wrap, leaving plenty draped over the edges. Spoon a third of the mixture into the dish and press it well down to eliminate any air pockets. Lay half the marinated duck breast strips lengthwise in the terrine and top with another third of the mixture. Repeat with the rest of the strips and finish with the pâté mixture, mounding the top in a dome. Lay a bay leaf on top and cover with the plastic wrap. Now add a lid or close covering of foil.

8 Set the terrine in a larger, deep roasting pan and pour in hot faucet water to come halfway up the sides of the dish, and put it in the preheated oven. Bake for 2 hours, or until a probe thermometer inserted into the center of the pâté reads 167°F.

9 Take the terrine from the oven and remove from the water bath. Set it in a larger dish and press it under a weight of about 2 pounds until it is cold. Refrigerate for 2 to 3 days to allow the maximum flavor to develop.

10 The day before serving the terrine, heat the jellied stock to the boiling point, simmer it for 5 minutes, and let cool until warm. In the meantime, turn the pâté out of its baking dish, peel off the plastic wrap, and dry the pâté by patting it with paper towels. Wash and dry the dish, then return the pâté to it. Dissolve the gelatin (if using) in the warm stock. Let the stock cool, but before it starts to set, pour it into the terrine. Decorate with a few juniper berries. Chill.

Tip
The terrine of duck cuts into attractive slices and, for that reason, is finished with jelly (aspic) rather than fat.

Creamy Chicken Liver Pâté

PREPARATION **30 MINUTES PLUS CHILLING**
COOKING **10 MINUTES**

Serves 6

10 tablespoons (1 ¼ sticks) unsalted
   butter
11½ ounces fresh chicken livers, cleaned
1 teaspoon chopped fresh tarragon
   leaves
⅓ cup finely chopped shallot
1 garlic clove, finely chopped
2 tablespoons sweet sherry
2 tablespoons mascarpone
salt and freshly ground black pepper

TO FINISH

3–4 tablespoons clarified butter or
   jellied stock (see page 182)
toast, to serve

This is a rich, smoothly spreadable pâté to be made, ideally, with fresh organic chicken livers. Present it in a single dish, or individual servings, with crunchy toasts. Sealing the surface with a slick of clarified butter (see page 181) or with jellied stock helps to preserve the pâté's pink tinge and stops it from graying.

1 Heat a sauté pan and add a walnut-size piece of butter. Add the chicken livers and tarragon leaves and sauté quickly, turning them, until they are colored on the outside but still pink in the center. Transfer to a blender or food processor.
2 Melt another wanut-size piece of butter and add the shallot and garlic. Sauté them for 2 to 3 minutes, until they are tender and translucent. Pour in the sherry and reduce until only a teaspoon remains. Add this mixture to the processor.

3 Add the mascarpone to the livers and season generously with salt and pepper. Process until the mixture is smooth, then let cool until the bowl is no longer warm to the touch. With the processor running, add the remaining butter, in 2 to 3 batches, and continue processing until the pâté is very smooth. Add salt and pepper to taste and divide the mixture among 6 small dishes. Cover and let chill.
4 As soon as the pâté is cold, run a thin layer of clarified butter or jellied stock over the surface. Let chill, then bring to room temperature and serve with toast.

Rustic Pork Terrine

A slice of this terrine served with a few homegrown salad leaves and crunchy cornichons makes a simple but deeply satisfying light lunch.

PREPARATION **1 HOUR**
COOKING **ABOUT 2 HOURS**

Makes about 3 pounds

2 pounds belly of pork

1 pound pig's liver

2 garlic cloves, finely chopped

⅔ cup finely chopped shallot

½ teaspoon ground mace

1 tablespoon sea salt

1 tablespoon whole green peppercorns, rinsed

6–7 tablespoons dry white wine

2 tablespoons brandy

5 ounces thinly sliced strips pancetta or bacon

1 bay leaf

1 Preheat the oven to 300°F.

2 Grind the pork and liver using the coarse or medium blade of a meat grinder and add the garlic, shallot, mace, salt, green peppercorns, wine, and brandy. Stir vigorously by hand or machine until the mixture starts to hold together in a sticky mass.

3 Cook (see page 180) a spoonful of the mixture to test for seasoning. If more is needed, mix it in thoroughly.

4 Line a 3-pound terrine with pancetta or bacon, leaving plenty draped over the edges to fold over the top. Spoon the mixture into the dish, pressing down well and finishing with a mounded top. Top with a bay leaf and fold the pancetta or bacon over. Now add a lid or close covering of foil.

5 Set the terrine in a roasting pan, pour in hot tap water to come halfway up the sides of the dish, and bake for about 2 hours, until a probe thermometer inserted into the center of the pâté reads 167°F.

6 Remove from the oven and the water bath. Set the terrine in a larger dish and press it under a weight of about 2 pounds until it is cold. Refrigerate for 2 to 3 days for maximum flavor to develop.

Mushroom Pâté

A few dried wild mushrooms add greatly to the flavor of this spreadable pâté made with a mixture of cultivated mushrooms. Though a large panful of fungi makes a relatively small quantity of pâté, what it lacks in bulk it delivers fully in taste.

PREPARATION **15 MINUTES PLUS SOAKING**
COOKING **15 MINUTES**

Serves 6
¼ ounces dried porcini or other wild mushrooms
6 tablespoons boiling water
2 tablespoons unsalted butter
⅓ cup finely chopped shallot
5 cups fresh mixed mushrooms, sliced
½ teaspoon salt
1 teaspoon fresh thyme leaves
2 tablespoons mascarpone
a dash of Tabasco sauce
1–2 teaspoons fresh lemon juice
1–2 teaspoons truffle oil (optional)

1 Soak the dried mushrooms in the boiling water for 30 minutes or more.
2 In a large sauté pan over lowish heat, melt the butter and sauté the shallot until it is soft. Raise the heat and add the sliced mushrooms, keeping them moving until they begin to fry and give off some moisture. Add the soaked mushrooms, their liquor, salt, and the thyme. Cook, stirring, over high heat until the mixture is completely dry.
3 Let cool completely before processing with the mascarpone, Tabasco, and a teaspoon each of lemon juice and truffle oil. Taste before adding more, if you like. Transfer to a sterilized kilner jar for storing.

Tip
Spread small crackers with a dab of mascarpone, a spoonful of mushroom pâté, and a sliver of Parmesan.

Potted Shrimp

Use tiny sweet brown shrimp if you can get hold of them or small North Atlantic shrimp.

PREPARATION **10 MINUTES PLUS CHILLING**
COOKING **2 TO 3 MINUTES**

Serves 2–3
10 tablespoons (1 ¼ sticks) unsalted butter
1 cup cooked small shrimp
a pinch of cayenne pepper
a squeeze of lemon juice
salt and freshly ground black pepper

1 Heat the butter over medium heat until melted and it stops sizzling—don't let it go brown. Skim away the froth. Pour the clear, golden (clarified) butter into a bowl, leaving behind the milky solids in the bottom of the pan.
2 Toss the shrimp in 1 tablespoon of the clarified butter and mix in the cayenne pepper and lemon juice. Check the seasoning.
3 Pack the shrimp into 2 to 3 ramekins and pour over the remaining butter. Let chill until set. Serve with toast. They will keep in the refrigerator for up to 5 days.

Potted Crabmeat

Spread on hot toast for a very pleasing supper or snack.

PREPARATION **15 MINUTES PLUS CHILLING**

Serves 2 to 3
1 cup picked fresh white and brown crabmeat
½ cup (1 stick) unsalted butter, softened
a pinch of cayenne pepper
1 teaspoon very finely chopped curly parsley
salt
a squeeze of lemon juice
clarified butter (see page 181)

1 Blend together the crabmeat, butter, cayenne pepper, and parsley. Season with salt and fresh lemon juice.
2 Divide between 2 to 3 small ramekins and cover with a thin layer of clarified butter. Let chill and use within 3 days.

INDEX

USEFUL ADDRESSES

BROADWAY PANHANDLER
65 East 8th Street
New York, NY 10003
Phone: 212-966-3434 /
866-COOKWARE (266-5972)
E-mail: pisales@
broadwaypanhandler.com
www.broadwaypanhandler.
com

BUTCHER & PACKER SUPPLY
COMPANY
1780 East 14 Mile Road
Madison Heights, MI 48071
Phone: 248-583-1250
www.butcher-packer.com

CANNING PANTRY
Highland Brands, LLC
19 N. 100 W.
Hyrum, UT 84319
Phone: 800-285-9044
www.canningpantry.com

KITCHEN KRAFTS
P.O. Box 442
Waukon, IA 52172
Phone: 800-298-5389 /
563-535-8000
E-mail: service@
kitchenkrafts.com
www.kitchenkrafts.com

LEENERS
9293 Olde Eight Road
Northfield, OH 44067
Phone: 800-543-3697
www.leeners.com

NEW YORK CAKE AND
BAKING DISTRIBUTOR
56 West 22nd Street
New York, NY 10021
Phone: 877-NYCAKE-8/
212-675-2253
www.nycake.com

THE SAUSAGE MAKER, INC.
1500 Clinton Street,
Building 123
Buffalo, NY 14206
Phone: 888-490-8525
E-mail: customerservice@
sausagemaker.com
www.sausagemaker.com

SUR LA TABLE
P.O. Box 840
Brownsburg, IN, 46112
Phone: 800-243-0852
www.surlatable.com
Please check Web site for
store locations

THE ULTIMATE BAKER
4917 East 2nd Avenue
Spokane Valley, WA 99212
Phone: 866-285-COOK (2665)
/ 509-954-5753
www.cooksdream.com

WECK JARS
450 Congress Parkway,
Suite E
Crystal Lake, IL 60014
Phone: 800-345-7381
www.weckcanning.com

WILLIAMS-SONOMA
Phone: 877-812-6235
www.williams-sonoma.com
Please check Web site for
store locations

ACKNOWLEDGMENTS

I would like to thank the following people for their help
with this book:

Tara Fisher for her wonderful photographs and Caroline
Reeves for her stunning and creative propping — a team
who was a true pleasure to work with and who made my
task of food styling so much easier. The team at Jacqui
Small: Kerenza Swift, Abi Waters, and Ashley Western for
pulling the whole book together so beautifully and being
so patient with me. The team at *Country Living* magazine —
just for being great. Most of all, my husband, Keith, and my
Mum and Dad for believing in me when I decided to retrain
at Leiths School of Food & Wine to realize my dream of
becoming a food writer. This book is for you. Thank you.